Expository Notes *from* Genesis and Exodus

Stuart Briscoe Expository Outlines

D. Stuart Briscoe

Baker Books

A Division of Baker Book House Co
Grand Rapids, Michigan 49516

Published by Baker Books
a division of Baker Book House Company
P.O. Box 6287, Grand Rapids, MI 49516-6287

Printed in the United States of America

ISBN 0-8010-1091-8

Contents

Part 2: Let's Do It God's Way

Preface

Outlines and skeletons are quite similar. Sermons without outlines tend to "flop around" like bodies without bones. But bones without flesh are not particularly attractive; neither are outlines without development. The outlines presented in this book are nothing more than skeletal for a very good reason. I have no desire to produce ready-made sermons for pastors who need to develop their own, but on the other hand I recognize that many busy pastors who find sermon preparation time hard to come by may at least use them as a foundation for their own study, meditation, and preaching. They can add flesh to the bones; they can add development to structure. All the sermons based on these outlines have been preached during the last twenty-two years of my ministry at Elmbrook Church in Milwaukee, Wisconsin, and as one might expect, they vary in style and substance—not to mention quality! I trust, however, that they all seek to teach the Word and apply it to the culture to which they were preached, and if they help another generation of preachers as they "preach the Word" I will be grateful.

Part 1

Beginnings from Genesis

1

God of Creation

Genesis 1

If you ever want to know how you're doing, check where you started, look at where you are, and figure out where you're going. Genesis means "beginning," so obviously this is a great place to start understanding everything significant.

I. Some preliminary remarks about Genesis
   A. Recognize the importance of Genesis
      1. Its own claims
      2. Its New Testament usage
   B. Realize the purpose of Genesis
      1. To explain the who and why
      2. Not the how and the when
   C. Resist the prejudices surrounding Genesis
      1. Scientific skepticism
      2. Theological tunnel vision

II. Some powerful revelations about God
  A. The God who originates
    1. His attributes
      a. His self-existence–in the beginning (see also John 1:1; 17:24)
      b. His self-sufficiency–*ʾĕlōhîm*, "Us"
      c. His self-determination–"Let us . . ."
    2. His actions
      a. His creative actions (Note: Hebrew *bārāʾ*)
        (1) Material creation (v. 1)
        (2) Relational creation (v. 21)
        (3) Spiritual creation (v. 27)
      b. His commissioning actions
        (1) The imparting of roles
        (2) The investing with significance
  B. The God who orders
    1. The power of his word–"God said . . . and there was . . ." (see also Heb. 11:3)
    2. The progression of his work
      a. From formlessness to form (Gen. 1:2–3)
      b. From form to fullness (vv. 20–30)
    3. The proportions of his will
      a. Man's insignificance in modern thinking
      b. Man's significance in ancient theology (vv. 26–28)
  C. The God who opines–"And God saw that it was good"

III. Some practical realities about goals (N.B. A created being has a sense of purpose and objective)
  A. A sense of wonder
  B. A participation in worship (Ps. 95; 136)
  C. An attitude of willingness

2

Man–God's Masterpiece

Having set the stage, the author of Genesis proceeds to bring man into the spotlight. Far from being an alternative and contradictory account of creation, Genesis 2 simply sharpens the focus on man–the masterpiece of God's creation.

    I. Man–a natural being
        A. Formed from dust (v. 7; 3:19)
        B. A living being (Hebrew *nepeš*) (v. 7; 1:20, 24)
        C. Part of the natural order
            1. Underemphasis–man is purely spiritual
            2. Overemphasis–man is superanimal

   II. Man–a spiritual being
        A. Capable of receiving what God gives (v. 7; see also John 20:22; 2 Tim. 3:16)
        B. Capable of responding to what God says (v. 16)

III. Man–a practical being
   A. Creation without man (v. 5)
   B. Man in creation (v. 15)

IV. Man–a rational being
   A. Understanding the workings of God (v. 19a)
   B. Undertaking a coworker's role with God
      (v. 19b)

V. Man–a moral being
   A. The privilege of being responsible
      1. Chosen to care for God's handiwork (v. 15)
      2. Chosen to obey God's directives (v. 16a)
      3. Chosen to observe God's limits (vv. 16b–17)
   B. The pressure of being responsible
      1. Not the unfortunate victim of determinism
         a. Genes
         b. Environment
      2. Not the unfettered lifestyle of animal instinct
      3. But the responsible position of choosing
         rightly (vv. 9, 17)

VI. Man–a social being
   A. A society that enjoys cooperation (v. 18)
   B. A society that honors commitment (v. 24)
   C. A society that respects concord (vv. 21–23)
   D. A society that appreciates contrast (v. 23)

VII. Man–a filial being
   A. A caring Father
   B. A loving child

3

Disaster in Eden

Genesis 3

Man is the world's greatest enigma. Capable of kindness and cruelty, creativity and destruction, he is a living contradiction. Evolutionary theory, which presupposes advance and improvement, cannot explain man, but Genesis 3 can. Made in the image of God, man fell. Disaster arrived in Eden.

 I. The conflict in Eden
   A. The ideal situation
      1. Man the object of God's love
      2. God the object of man's love
         a. The discerning mind of man
         b. The desiring emotions of man
         c. The deciding will of man
      3. Love the result of intelligent choice—obey or disobey
   B. The infamous temptation
      1. The serpent's seduction of Eve

      a. Integrity of God doubted (v. 1)
      b. Intentions of God denied (v. 4)
      c. Independence of God desired (v. 5)
      d. Instructions of God disobeyed (v. 6)
   2. The woman's seduction of man
      a. Loyalty confused by love
      b. Decision clouded by desire
  C. The inevitable disintegration
   1. Spiritual disintegration (v. 8)
   2. Personal disintegration
      a. Guilt
      b. Shame
      c. Fear
      d. Escape
   3. Social disintegration
      a. Evasion of responsibility (v. 11)
      b. Transference of guilt (v. 12)

II. The consequences on earth
  A. The struggles of the serpent (vv. 14–15)
   1. Humiliation
   2. Enmity
   3. Defeat
  B. The struggles of the woman (v. 16)
   1. With children
   2. With men
  C. The struggles of the man (vv. 17–19)
   1. With economic survival
   2. With a sense of futility

III. The conclusion in eternity
  A. The Seed will triumph (v. 15; Rom. 5:12–21; 1 Cor. 15:20–28)
  B. The serpent will be defeated (Rev. 20)

4

The Human Race

Genesis 4

The human race, numbering more than four billion persons, populates a tiny planet in the vastness of space. Scripture speaks clearly about the significance of the race and the special place it holds in the purposes of God. The race needs to be seen, therefore, in the light of revelation.

    I. The derivation of the human race
        A. Derived from a volitional union—sex a decision
        B. Derived from a sexual union—"one flesh," "his wife"
        C. Derived from a biological union—"conceived"
        D. Derived from a spiritual union—"help of the Lord"
        E. Derived from a moral union—"Cain"= "acquired"

    II. The dedication of the human race
        A. Dedication to love
           1. Spouse to spouse

    2. Parent to child
    3. Child to child
  B. Dedication to labor
    1. Cain–agricultural labor (v. 2)
    2. Jabal–pastoral labor (v. 20)
    3. Jubal–artistic labor (v. 21)
    4. Tubal–industrial labor (v. 22)
  C. Dedication to the Lord
    1. Abel offering to the Lord (v. 4)
      a. First born
      b. Fat portions
    2. Seth, Enosh honoring the Lord (v. 26)

III. The deviation of the human race
  A. The explanation of this deviation
    1. The presence of sin–crouching (v. 7)
    2. The purpose of sin–desiring
    3. The power of sin–mastering
  B. The expression of this deviation
    1. In terms of love
      a. Murder (v. 8)
      b. Polygamy (v. 19)
      c. My brother's keeper? (v. 9)
    2. In terms of labor–abuses of II.B.
    3. In terms of the Lord
      a. Reticence in worship (v. 3)
      b. Resentment of rebuke (v. 6)
      c. Resistance of God (v. 6)
      d. Refusal of judgment (v. 13)
    4. Ridicule of righteousness (vv. 23–24)

5

Life and Death

Genesis 5

The fifth chapter of Genesis is a genealogy of one line of the human race from Adam to Noah. At first sight it may appear to hold little interest to anyone other than a historian or a theologian. But notice one recurring theme: "He lived . . . then he died." The human race has always grappled with these two things and so must we.

I. Coming to grips with life
   A. Living the ideal life (vv. 1–2)
      1. Living the created life
      2. Living the childlike life
      3. Living the creative life
      4. Living the consecrated life
      5. Living the called life
   B. Living the forfeited life
      1. Living the spoiled life (cf. vv. 1–3)
      2. Living the sorrowful life
      3. Living the strained life (v. 29)

   C. Living the extraordinary life
      1. Walking with God (vv. 22–24)
         a. In agreement with him (Amos 3:3)
         b. In obedience to him (Deut. 10:12)
         c. In reverence for him (Acts 9:31)
         d. In humility before him (Micah 6:8)
         e. In openness to him (1 John 1:7)
      2. Pleasing God (Heb. 11:5–6)
         a. Impossible in the flesh (Rom. 8:8)
         b. Impossible without faith
      3. Identifying with God (Jude 14–15)

  II. Coming to grips with death
    A. Dying a spiritual death (Gen. 3:3)
      1. Termination of a spiritual relationship
      2. Deterioration of spiritual resources
      3. Disintegration of spiritual reality
    B. Dying a physical death
      1. The inevitability of physical death
      2. The universality of physical death
      3. The immensity of physical death
         a. The wages of sin (Rom. 6:23)
         b. The end of life (Eccles. 12:5–7)
         c. The entrance to eternity (Heb. 9:27)
    C. Dying an eternal death (Rev. 20:11–15)

 III. Coming to grips with life after death
    A. The possibilities as illustrated by Enoch
       (Gen. 5:24)
    B. The certainties as enunciated by Christ
       (John 14:1–3)
    C. The practicalities as demonstrated by Paul
       (Phil. 1:21)

6

The Character of God

Genesis 6

Recent years have witnessed a great development in man's knowledge of himself, his society, and his environment. There is, however, an urgent need for man to develop his knowledge of God. This can be done only through careful attention to God's self-revelation. God's dealings with the human race in the days of Noah are extremely valuable in this respect.

I. God's principles
   A. The creation principle (v. 7)
      1. Existence the result of divine choice
      2. Purpose the product of divine decision
   B. The identification principle
      1. Identification through difference (kinds)
      2. Identification through definition (limits)—
         man is limited to:
         a. Obedience
         b. Dependence
         c. Consequence

II. God's perspective
  A. Increasing disobedience (v. 5)
    1. How great
    2. Every
    3. Only
    4. All the time
  B. Independent attitudes
    1. The choices of the "sons of God" (v. 2)
    2. The contending of the Spirit of God (v. 3)
  C. Inevitable destruction
    1. Destruction through encroaching corruption (vv. 11–12)
    2. Destruction through divine intervention (v. 7)

III. God's pain
  A. God's unchanging stability (see 2 Sam. 15:29, 35)
  B. God's unending sensitivity (Gen. 6:6)

IV. God's pleasure
  A. God delights to dispense grace (v. 8)
  B. God delights in those who will receive his grace (v. 9)–shown by:
    1. Witness among men–righteousness
    2. Wholeheartedness towards God
    3. Walk with God

V. God's provision
  A. The idea (v. 14)
  B. The idealness (vv. 15–16)

VI. God's patience
  A. Allowing human cooperation (v. 14)
  B. Permitting human repentance (see 2 Peter 2:5)

VII. God's promise
  A. God's choice to make covenants (v. 18)
  B. God's commitment to the covenants he makes

7

A Man of Faith

Genesis 7

The story of the Genesis flood raises monumental problems of interpretation and integration, but in the midst of this stands a man whose life honored God and gave clear direction to a lost generation. Noah lived the faith life.

    I. Faith—a response to revelation
       A. What God revealed about himself
       B. What God revealed about his creation
       C. What God revealed about his intentions

   II. Faith—a relationship of trust
       A. A walk that continued
       B. A walk that persevered
       C. A walk that contrasted

  III. Faith—a readiness to obey
       A. Despite the immensity of the task

B. Despite the enormity of the responsibility

C. Despite the incongruity of the situation

IV. Faith—a release of blessing

    A. Blessing to himself—heir of righteousness (Heb. 11:7)

    B. Blessing to his family (Gen. 7:13)

    C. Blessing to his community—preacher of righteousness

V. Faith—a resource of power

    A. Power to take decisive actions

    B. Power to make incisive declarations

    C. Power to display alternative attitudes

VI. Faith—a rebuke to unfaithfulness

    A. He condemned his world (Heb. 11:7)

    B. He challenged the status quo

VII. Faith—a reminder to the faithful

    A. A reminder to be serious (Matt. 24:37–42)

    B. A reminder to be faithful

    C. A reminder to be ready

8
The New Creation

Genesis 8

God's dealings with the human race in the time of Noah demonstrated many aspects of his unchanging character and purposes. After the destruction of the old creation, he introduced Noah and his family to "the new creation." This theme of a new creation is repeated in Scripture for our edification.

I. The new creation in the past
   A. The entrance to the new creation
      1. Through the grace of God (v. 1)
      2. Through the judgment of God (v. 2)
      3. Through the provision of God
      4. Through faith in God
      5. Through obedience to God (vv. 16–18)
   B. The enjoyment of the new creation
      1. The excitement of exploration
         a. An inquiring mind (v. 6)

  b. A persistent attitude (vv. 6–10)
  c. An intelligent approach (v. 11)
  2. The discipline of delay
    a. Sin leaves scars that heal slowly
    b. Judgment brings destruction that drains slowly (v. 5)
    c. God has plans that move slowly (v. 15)
  3. The sweetness of sacrifice
    a. Noah's generous attitude (v. 20)
    b. God's gracious acceptance (v. 21)
  4. The certainty of commitment
    a. Dependent on God's promise (v. 21)
    b. Despite man's perversity (v. 21b)

II. The new creation in the present (2 Cor. 5:17–21)
  A. The entrance in Christ
  B. The enjoyment
    1. Recognize "the old has gone" (Gen. 8:17)
    2. Realize "the new has come" (v. 17)
    3. Relay the good news (v. 20)

III. The new creation in prophecy (2 Peter 3:3–18)
  A. The prediction of final judgment (vv. 3–7)
  B. The promise of new heavens and earth (vv. 12–13)
  C. The preparation for these events (vv. 11, 14)

9

Human Dignity

Genesis 9

After the tragic events of the flood, Noah and his family were reminded by God of their special place in his economy and the dignity he had conferred upon them. They were to learn how to behave in a way compatible with this privilege.

   I. The protection of human dignity
       A. By understanding:
           1. Special creation (v. 6b)
           2. Special commission (vv. 1b–3)
           3. Special covenant (v. 9)
           4. Special consecration (v. 1a)
           5. Special communication (v. 17)
       B. By undertaking:
           1. Personal evaluations
           2. Individual relations

  3. Societal positions
   a. Political
   b. Economic
   c. Academic

 II. The prostitution of human dignity
  A. The causes of this prostitution
   1. Special creation has been dismissed
   2. Special commission has been diluted
   3. Special covenant has been ignored
   4. Special consecration has been rejected
   5. Special communication has been disobeyed
  B. The characteristics of this prostitution
   1. The cheapness of human life
    a. The incidence of violence
    b. The absence of justice (vv. 4–6)
   2. The casualness of human relationships
    a. The breaking of covenants
    b. The breakdown of commitment
   3. The corruptness of moral standards
    a. The absence of self-respect (v. 21)
    b. The abdication of self-control (v. 21)

 III. The promotion of human dignity
  A. By proclaiming God's grace to man (v. 1)
  B. By emulating the sons' attitude to the father (v. 23)
  C. By sharing Christ's concern for the under-privileged (v. 25; see also Luke 4:18–19)

10

Untied Nations

Genesis 10

[ver since the flood, the human race has been growing both in numbers and in national identity. Efforts to unite the nations have shown them to be more untied than united. How did this condition develop, what can be done about it, and where will it all end?

I. The formation of the nations
   A. The personality of Nimrod
      1. His power as a leader (v. 8)
      2. His prowess as a man (v. 9a)
      3. His popularity with the people (v. 9b)
      4. His progressiveness as an innovator (vv. 10–11)
   B. The philosophy of Babel (11:1–4)
      1. Self-promotion
      2. Self-protection
      3. Self-propagation
   C. The perspective of God (11:5–9)

      1. God's interest in man's activities
      2. God's interpretation of man's intentions
      3. God's intervention in man's affairs
        a. He confused their communications
          (11:7–8)
        b. He confounded their community

II. The frustrations of the nations
    A. The identity of a nation (10:5, 20, 31)
      1. Geographical identity–"territories"
      2. Social identity–"clans"
      3. Political identity–"nations"
      4. Cultural identity–"language"
      5. Ancestral identity–"sons"
    B. The interaction of the nations
      1. The formation of alliance
      2. The perpetuation of antagonism
    C. The internals of a nation
      1. Confusion about identity
      2. Conflict about interaction

III. The future of the nations
    A. Continuing alienation (Ps. 2:1–3; Matt. 24:7)
    B. Continuing evangelization (Matt. 24:14)
      1. From Babel to Pentecost (Acts 2:5–11)
      2. From earth to glory (Rev. 5:9–10)
    C. Eventual subjugation (Ps. 2:8–9)

11

God and Abram

Genesis 11

Having sketched God's activity from the beginning to the founding of the nations, Genesis concentrates on God's special dealings with a man called Abram and his descendants.

I. The call
  A. It was distinctive
    1. God's selectivity
      a. Creation, not chaos
      b. Human, not machine
      c. Partnership, not dictatorship
      d. Abram, not another
    2. Humanity's suitability
      a. Abram more suitable than Terah (vv. 31–32)
      b. Sarai more suitable than Milcah (v. 30)
  B. It was disruptive
    1. Invisible God for moon god

        2. Canaan for Ur
          a. Primitive for sophisticated
          b. Rural for urban
        3. Uncertainty for certainty (see Heb. 11:8)
     C. It was decisive
        1. It was pointed–"Leave and go" (Gen. 12:1)
        2. It was permanent–"The Lord had said"

  II. The choice
     A. To obey or disobey
        1. God desires obedience
        2. God deserves obedience
        3. God demands obedience
        4. Man is free to disregard, dismiss, and disobey
     B. To trust or distrust (Heb. 11:8–11)
        1. Trust in a future reality (v. 10)
        2. Trust in a faithful God (v. 11)
        3. Man is free to think faith too risky, costly, or childish

 III. The conclusion
     A. God still uses people
     B. God still calls individuals
     C. God still expects obedience
     D. God still merits faith
     E. God still tolerates dissenters

12

Faith

Genesis 12

The relationship between God and Abram required that God should be faithful and Abram exercise faith. The ways in which the relationship flourished on this basis are clearly explained in Scripture for our edification.

I. The experience of faith
   A. Revelation
      1. The Lord had appeared (v. 7)
      2. The Lord had said (v. 1)
         a. What Abram should do
         b. What he (God) would do (vv. 2–3)
            (1) I will make you
            (2) I will bless you
            (3) I will honor you
            (4) I will support you
            (5) I will use you
            (6) I will surprise you (v. 7)
            (7) I will give you

B. Recognition
  1. The faithfulness of God—what grounds did he have?
  2. The truthfulness of his word—what evidence did he have?
C. Reaction
  1. "So Abram left . . ." (v. 4)
  2. Subordinating the secular to the spiritual
  3. Substituting the unknown for the known

II. The extremities of faith
  A. When faith adds up the cost (v. 1)
  B. When faith confronts the opposition (v. 6)– "The Canaanites were in the land."
  C. When faith faces up to danger (vv. 11–13)
  D. When faith meets famine (v. 10)

III. The expressions of faith
  A. Readiness to take a stand (v. 7)
    1. An altar confirming his position
    2. An altar contradicting the opposition
  B. Willingness to take a step (vv. 6, 9, 10)
    1. The initial step from Ur
    2. The continual steps in Canaan
  C. Eagerness to make a statement (v. 8)
    1. Calling on the name of the Lord
    2. Continuing in the Way of the Lord

13

Facing Up to Reality

Genesis 13

Abram was a man of faith, but that does not mean he was a stranger to reality. In fact, his faith put him in touch with ultimate reality, which he demonstrated by the way he faced up to circumstances.

  I. Facing up to failure (vv. 1–4)
   A. Recognizing failure, Abram:
     1. Retraced his steps
     2. Returned to basics
     3. Refreshed his soul
     4. Renewed his commitment

 II. Facing up to friction (vv. 5–9)
   A. Someone has to make a move because:
     1. Matters only get worse
     2. Causes don't go away
     3. Problems don't solve themselves

    B. Someone has to make an appeal
      1. To what we have in common
      2. To what we must share
    C. Someone has to make a concession
      1. If nobody moves, nothing changes
      2. If somebody moves, someone follows

III. Facing up to facts (vv. 10–18)
    A. Some situations won't work out
      1. The details are all wrong (v. 6)
      2. The arrangement was never right (12:1)
      3. The decision must be made
    B. Some people will disappoint you
      1. Their values are different
      2. Their choices are defective
    C. Some things won't change
      1. God's call survives diversions
      2. God's promises transcend disappointments
      3. God's intentions ignore delays

14

Getting Involved

Genesis 14

Abram's world was complex. Numerous forces for good and evil were at work all around him. He could not isolate himself from the situations that surrounded him. The degree to which he got involved with his world as a man of faith is enlightening.

I. Abram's involvement with Sodom
   A. Sodom's situation
      1. Spiritual depravity–"against the Lord" (13:13)
      2. Moral degeneration–"sinned greatly" (13:13)
      3. Social deprivation–deprived of:
         a. Freedom
         b. Property
         c. Justice
   B. Abram's options
      1. Total isolation

       a. The reasons
         (1) It's none of my business
         (2) They got what they deserved
         (3) The odds are too great
         (4) What about me?
         (5) I'm too involved already
       b. The results
         (1) Injustice not countered
         (2) Suffering not alleviated
    2. Total identification
       a. Accepting Sodom's philosophy
       b. Bearing Sodom's burdens
       c. Adopting Sodom's lifestyle
  C. Abram's solution
    1. Total isolation is unthinkable
    2. Total identification is impossible
    3. Total involvement is imperative
       a. In meeting the needs
         (1) Facing a challenge (vv. 14–16)
         (2) Utilizing resources
       b. In maintaining the difference
         (1) A matter of principle (vv. 21–23)
         (2) A matter of practicality (v. 24)

II. Abram's involvement with Salem
  A. Salem's unique attributes
    1. Its name
       a. "Salem"="peace"
       b. "Jerusalem"="founding or possession of peace"
    2. Its king
       a. "Melchizedek"="king of righteousness"
       b. Type of Christ (see Heb. 7)
    3. Its God
       a. "ʾēl ʿelyôn"="God Most High"
       b. Creator, possessor of all

B. Abram's attitude
   1. The plunderer accepts gifts (v. 18)
   2. The patriarch receives a blessing (v. 19)
   3. The warrior presents tithes (v. 20)
   4. The Jehovah worshiper honors ʾēl ʿelyôn (v. 22)

15

The Promises of God

Genesis 15

The special relationship that God enjoyed with Abram was characterized by the promises of God and the ability of Abram to respond to them. All spiritual relationships operate on the same basis. We need, therefore, to continually alert ourselves to the promises and examine our responses.

    I. The promises of God banish fear (vv. 1–3)
       A. God's reassurance to Abram (v. 1)
          1. Its timing–"after this" (v. 1)
          2. Its content
             a. A reminder of God's presence
             b. A reminder of God's provision
          3. Its challenge–"don't be afraid"
       B. Abram's request to God (vv. 2–3)
          1. The basis of certainty
          2. The degree of uncertainty
          3. The need for clarification

II. The promises of God promote faith (vv. 4–6)
    A. The specific aspects of God's promise
        1. The promise of offspring
        2. The elimination of confusion (v. 4)
    B. The special elements of Abram's faith (see Rom. 4:17–25)
        1. Confidence in a person
        2. Conversant with problems
        3. Consistent in progress
        4. Convinced of promise
    C. The significant application of this incident
        1. Faith, not works, leads to righteousness (Rom. 4)
        2. Grace, not law, procures justification (Gal. 3)

III. The promises of God unveil the future (Gen. 15:7–21)
    A. The certainty of God's covenant
        1. The ancient ritual (vv. 9–11)
        2. The solemn setting (v. 12)
        3. The striking appearance (v. 17)
    B. The web of God's will
        1. He had to grant Abram the land (v. 13)
        2. He had to get Israel ready (v. 14)
        3. He had to give the Amorites a chance (v. 16)
    C. The particulars of God's prediction
        1. He will do what he says
        2. He will take the time necessary
        3. He will treat people justly
        4. He will be honored

16

Making Mistakes

Genesis 16

Alexander Pope said, "To err is human, to forgive divine." Human beings give ample evidence of the accuracy of the observation. Abram and Sarai are no exception, and we can profit greatly if we learn from their mistakes.

I. Making mistakes (vv. 1–4)
   A. Mistakes have their causes
      1. When the importance of the desired end is exaggerated
      2. When impatience for results is uncontrolled
      3. When impulses are not governed by wisdom
      4. When the impact of contemporary thought is great
      5. When the immutability of God's law is disregarded
      6. When impotence takes the place of conviction

    B. Mistakes have their consequences
       1. Human beings are responsible
       2. Natural laws produce results
       3. Moral principles promise consequences

II. Making mistakes worse (vv. 5–6)
    A. Bad attitudes make matters worse
       1. Hagar's attitudes
         a. Unbecoming pride
         b. Undisguised disdain
       2. Sarai's attitudes
         a. Unashamed self-centeredness
         b. Unfounded self-justification
         c. Unspiritual self-righteousness
       3. Abram's attitudes
         a. Unimpressive passivity
         b. Unconcerned evasion
    B. Wrong actions make matters worse
       1. Sarai tried to get even
       2. Abram tried to get out of it
       3. Hagar tried to get away from it

III. Making something out of mistakes (vv. 7–15)
    A. Recognize something about God in the situation
       1. God's compassion for the underprivileged
       2. God's commitment to his principles
         a. He'll bless our mistakes
         b. But he won't change his plans
    B. Realize something about yourself
       1. Hagar needed to return
       2. Abram needed to respond
       3. Sarai needed to receive
    C. Respond to God's revelation
       1. Hagar saw the one who sees—"Beer Lahai Roi"
       2. Abram knew the one who knows—"Ishmael"

17

Commitment–God's Way

Genesis 17

The early chapters of Genesis reveal God as a covenant-making Deity. The essence of the covenant is God's commitment to mankind and the necessity for a committed response from mankind.

    I. The concept of the covenant (Heb. *bĕrît*)
       A. The equality aspect
          1. The *bĕrît* of friendship (1 Sam. 23:18)
          2. The *bĕrît* of trade (1 Kings 20:34)
          3. The *bĕrît* of marriage (Prov. 2:16–17)
       B. The inequality aspect
          1. The suzerainty *bĕrît* (Josh. 9)
             a. Guaranteed by the stronger
             b. For the good of the weaker
       C. The integrity aspect
          1. The making of a promise (Gen. 15:18)
          2. The maledictory aspect

   II. The content of the covenant
      A. The introduction
         1. "I am God Almighty"—*ʾēl šadday* (17:1)
         2. The covenant is dependent on my ability
      B. The promises—"As for me" (vv. 2–8)
         1. I will give you descendants
         2. I will give you land
         3. I will be your God
      C. The challenge—"As for you" (v. 9)
         1. The challenge to believe (15:6)
         2. The challenge to be wholehearted (17:1)
         3. The challenge to accept the difference
            (vv. 5, 15)
         4. The challenge to obey (vv. 9–14)

  III. The consequences of the covenant
      A. The extent of the promises
         1. Greater than lineal descent—"many nations"
         2. Broader than geographical boundaries
      B. The depth of the commitment
         1. The maledictory aspect
         2. The covenant in my blood (1 Cor. 11:25–26)
      C. The reality of the response
         1. Humbleness of attitude (Gen. 17:3, 17)
         2. Readiness of faith
         3. Wholeheartedness of walk
         4. Fullness of obedience
            a. Moral
            b. Ceremonial

18

Big Questions about God

Genesis 18

After the establishing of the covenant, Abraham was visited by three men, whom he discovered to be Jehovah and two angels. The surprise visit resulted in a fascinating dialogue between the Lord and his friend. Perhaps the most helpful parts of the conversation were the questions that were raised and the answers given.

  I. A question of divine ability (vv. 1–15): "Is anything too hard for the Lord?" (v. 14)
     A. The circumstances leading to the question
        1. The Lord had revealed himself as Lord
        2. Abraham had recognized him as Lord
           a. Worshiping the Lord (v. 2)
           b. Welcoming the Lord (vv. 3–7)
           c. Waiting on the Lord (v. 8)
        3. The Lord had reiterated his intentions as Lord
        4. Sarah had laughed at the Word of the Lord (v. 12)

B. The concerns behind the question
   1. How clear was her conception of God?
   2. How great was her grasp of God?
   3. How deep was her devotion to God?
C. The challenge within the question
   1. The challenge to arrive at a conclusion
      (e.g., Acts 26:8)
   2. The challenge to develop consistency
      (e.g., John 11:38-39)

II. A question of divine strategy (Gen. 18:16-22):
    "Shall I hide from Abraham what I am about to
    do?" (v. 17)
    A. God's recognition of Sodom's iniquity
    B. God's resolve to implement his purposes
    C. God's relationship with Abraham
       1. A relationship of friendship
       2. A relationship of partnership (vv. 18-19)
          a. Abraham's part
          b. God's promise
       3. A relationship of stewardship
          a. Abraham's knowledge of God's action
          b. Abraham's responsibility to teach and
             warn

III. A question of divine integrity (vv. 23-33): "Will
     not the Judge of all the earth do right?" (v. 25)
     A. Man's unusual sense of morality
     B. God's unique characteristic of righteousness
     C. The Judge's unswerving commitment to justice
        1. Including mercy
        2. Incorporating wrath
        3. Involving patience
        4. Integrating grace

19

The Significance of Sodom

Genesis 19

Few cities have earned the notoriety of Sodom, and none has suffered more. The circumstances that led to the city's downfall and the consequences of such a catastrophe are repeated literally from Genesis to Revelation. Such coverage demands our attention.

I. The condition of Sodom's society
   A. The attractiveness of the vicinity (Gen. 13:10)
   B. The air of normality (Luke 17:28)
   C. The abuse of prosperity (Ezek. 16:49–50)
   D. The absence of morality (2 Peter 2:7–8)
   E. The attraction of perversity (Gen. 19:4–9)
   F. The attitude of immodesty (Isa. 3:9)

II. The consequences of Sodom's sin
   A. From Lot's perspective
      1. He was entangled
         a. His initial choice

      b. His gradual involvement
      c. His ineffectual witness
      d. His crucial error
      e. His continual struggle
      f. His final humiliation
    2. His wife was engulfed
    3. His sons-in-law were entertained
    4. His daughters were enthralled
  B. From the Lord's perspective
    1. His commitment to righteousness
      a. Being true to his own character
      b. Being true to man's choice
        Note: Judgment is God's finalizing of man's deciding
    2. His commitment to patience
    3. His commitment to mercy

III. The conviction of Sodom's significance
  A. Conviction concerning Sodom's judgment
    1. The reality of God's judgment
    2. The responsibility of added knowledge (Matt. 11:23)
  B. Conviction concerning Lot's weakness
    1. A good start
    2. A poor finish
  C. Conviction concerning Lot's wife (Luke 17:32)
    1. A great opportunity
    2. A terrible tragedy

20

The Danger of Underestimating

Genesis 20

E ver since Eve underestimated the serpent, human beings have made the same mistake. Goliath underestimated David, the Israelites underestimated Ai, Chamberlain underestimated Hitler, the Americans underestimated the Vietnamese, and Abraham underestimated just about everything. Only God averted a disaster.

I. The danger of underestimating personal characteristics
   A. Abraham's deep-rooted weakness
      1. Not afraid to step out in faith
      2. Not afraid to confront four kings
      3. Not afraid to challenge God
      4. But afraid he might be killed because of Sarah
   B. Abraham's long-established principle

    1. Born in the land of the Chaldeans (v. 13)
    2. Nurtured in the land of the Egyptians (Gen. 12)
    3. Practiced in the land of the Philistines (Gen. 20:2)
  C. Abraham's high-minded attitude
    1. He assumed his own superiority
    2. He assumed Philistinian inferiority (v. 11)
  D. Abraham's broad-based interpretation
    1. His interpretation of love
    2. His interpretation of truth

 II. The danger of underestimating spiritual considerations
  A. The consideration of spiritual exhaustion
    1. Anticlimax follows climax (see Gen. 12)
    2. Weakness follows strength (see Gen. 19)
  B. The consideration of spiritual sickness
    1. What about the promises? Spiritual amnesia
    2. Does only Abraham count in this world? Spiritual myopia

III. The danger of underestimating special circumstances
  A. Abraham knew the danger of living among Philistines
  B. Abraham forgot the danger of ignoring history

IV. The danger of underestimating practical consequences
  A. The consequences of lost faith for Abimelech
  B. The consequences of lost virtue for Sarah
  C. The consequences of lost credibility for Abraham
  D. The consequences of a lost Savior for the world

V. The danger of underestimating divine control
   A. God's control of Abimelech's dreams
      (Gen. 20:3)
   B. God's control of Abimelech's action (v. 6)
   C. God's control of Sarah's position (v. 6)
   D. God's control of Abraham's ministry (v. 7)
   E. God's control of Abimelech's family (v. 17)

21

Laughter

Genesis 21

After many dramatic incidents and divine reminders, the promised child, Isaac, was born. His name means "laughter," which according to some is "the best medicine" but to others is sheer poison.

I. Lots of laughs
   A. The laughter of disbelief (Gen. 18:12)
      1. Disbelief through ignorance (John 3)
      2. Disbelief through superior attitude (Matt. 9:23–25)
      3. Disbelief through denial (Gen. 12)
   B. The laughter of discovery (Gen. 21:6)
      1. Discovery of God's grace (v. 1)
      2. Discovery of God's provision
      3. Discovery of God's timing (v. 2; cf. 2 Kings 7; Acts 2)
      4. Discovery of God's power
      5. Discovery of God's promise

C. The laughter of derision (Gen. 21:9)
   1. Deriding what cannot be explained
   2. Deriding what will not be accepted
      (e.g., Matt. 27:27–31)
   3. Deriding what is not feared
D. The laughter of discord (Gal. 4:21–31)
   1. The application of the allegory
   2. The differentiation between the sons
   3. The antagonism between the systems
E. The laughter of dissipation (Eccles. 7:1–6)
   1. The avoidance of reality
   2. The attention of fantasy
F. The laughter of distraction (Eccles. 3:4)
   1. The necessity for relaxation
   2. The possibility of recreation

II. Limits of laughter
   A. The time for laughter to stop
      1. The challenge that stopped Sarah laughing
         (Gen. 18:15)
      2. The circumstances that stopped Abraham
         laughing (Gen. 21:11)
      3. The consequences that stopped Ishmael
         laughing (v. 17)
   B. The time for laughter to start (Ps. 126)
      1. When God's blessing is appreciated
         (vv. 1–3)
      2. When God's blessing is anticipated (vv. 4–6)

III. He who laughs last
   A. Don't forget the laughter of God (Ps. 2)
   B. Don't dare laugh at God (Gal. 6:7)
   C. Don't laugh when you should be mourning
      (Luke 6:25)
   D. Don't mourn when you should be laughing
      (Luke 6:21)

22

Faith's High Point

Genesis 22

Abraham's faith, like everybody's faith, waxed and waned. Sometimes his actions were examples of superb trust and confidence; other times he demonstrated nothing more than his own fallibility. On Mount Moriah he reached the high point.

    I. The incident as a test
       A. What was the origin of the test?
          1. It was not Abraham being influenced by Canaanites
          2. It was not the devil trying to hinder God's work
          3. It was God putting his servant to the test (v. 1)
       B. What was the objective of the test?
          1. Faith needs to be matured (James 1:2–4)
          2. Faith needs to be expressed (James 2:14–24)
       C. What was the outcome of the test?

1. His faith was stronger than natural affection (Gen. 22:2)
2. His faith was richer than cherished possessions
3. His faith was greater than personal ambition
4. His faith was more powerful than intellectual rationalization
   a. Question: "What's going to happen?" Answer: "We will come back to you." (v. 5)
   b. Question: "Where is the lamb?" (v. 7) Answer: "God himself will provide." (v. 8)
   c. Question: "What about the promise?" Answer: "God could raise the dead." (Heb. 11:17–19)

II. The incident as a triumph
   A. A triumph of divine intervention
      1. God's sense of timing (Gen. 22:10–13)
         a. The knife in the hand
         b. The ram in the thicket
   B. A triumph of divine interpretation (v. 12)
      1. The willingness was what counted
      2. The fear of God was demonstrated
   C. A triumph of divine information (vv. 16–18)
      1. The divine intention reiterated
      2. The divine name invoked (Heb. 6:13–18)

III. The incident as a type
   A. Abraham as a type of the Father
      1. "You have not withheld from me your son." (Gen. 22:12)
      2. "He that spared not his only son." (Rom. 8:32)
   B. Isaac as a type of the Servant

    1. "He bound his son Isaac and laid him on the altar." (v. 9)
    2. "He was led like a lamb to the slaughter." (Isa. 53:7–10)

C. Ram as a type of substitute
    1. "A burnt offering instead of his son." (Gen. 22:13)
    2. "Christ died for our sins." (1 Cor. 15:3)

23

Coping with Death

Genesis 23

After a long and eventful life, Sarah died at the ripe old age of 127. Abraham's handling of this traumatic event is helpful, as it shows the man who lived by faith coping with death.

    I. Coping with dying (see Eccles. 12:1–8)
       A. The reality of diminishing capabilities (Note Paul's statement in 2 Cor. 4:16–18)
         1. Physical deterioration
           a. Beauty
           b. Sexuality
           c. Vigor
         2. Mental deterioration
           a. Learning
           b. Retaining

      3. Emotional deterioration
        a. Fearfulness
        b. Worry
      4. Social deterioration
        a. Redundancy
        b. Loneliness
   B. The possibility of increasing infirmities
      1. The problem of pain
      2. The frustration of restriction
      3. The loss of independence
   C. The inevitability of impending separations
      1. The termination of relationships
      2. The sense of loss
      3. The preparation of life

 II. Coping with death
   A. The inevitability of death (Heb. 9:27)
   B. The immensity of death
      1. The wages of sin
        a. Physical
        b. Spiritual
        c. Eternal
      2. The entrance to eternity
        a. Heaven
        b. Hell
      3. The individuality of death
        a. For me
        b. For mine

III. Coping with bereavement
   A. Grief should be expected
      1. The sense of loss
      2. The fact of finality
   B. Grief must be expressed
      1. An expression of shock
      2. An expression of emotion

3. An expression of desolation
4. An expression of panic
5. An expression of guilt

C. Grief must not be extended
1. Hope is the Christian factor (1 Thess. 4:13)
2. Acceptance is a practical necessity
3. Adjustment is a realistic goal

24

Commitment

Genesis 24

It has been said that the nation is experiencing a "crisis of confidence." This is probably the result of a crisis of commitment!

   I. Reaching a conviction about commitment
      A. The scarcity of conviction
         1. The world is changing
         2. The society is corrupt
         3. The commitment is costly
      B. The necessity of commitment
         1. The nature of God declares commitment (v. 7)
            a. Commitment to his principles
            b. Commitment to his purposes
            c. Commitment to his promises
            d. Commitment to his people

      2. The survival of society demands
        commitment
        a. Society must believe something about
          itself
        b. Society must do something about its belief
      3. The heart of man desires commitment
        a. A sense of worth
        b. A sense of purpose

  II. Recognizing the characteristics of commitment
     A. A commitment to Providence
       1. The goodness of God (v. 7)
       2. The guidance of God (vv. 12–14)
     B. A commitment to principle
       1. Abraham's commitment to separation
         (vv. 3–4)
        a. Firm
        b. Flexible
       2. Eliezer's commitment to integrity (v. 9)
        a. Saying what he would do
        b. Doing what he said
       3. Rebekah's commitment to purity (v. 16)
        a. Recognizing the right
        b. Resisting the wrong
       4. Isaac's commitment to meditation (v. 63)
     C. A commitment to performance
       1. Performance that succeeds (v. 56)
       2. Performance that completes (v. 56)
       3. Performance that exceeds (v. 19)
       4. Performance that enthuses (v. 20)
     D. A commitment to people
       1. Eliezer's commitment to Abraham
       2. Rebekah's commitment to Isaac
       3. Deborah's commitment to Rebekah

 III. Reaping the consequences of commitment
     A. Personal enrichment

      1. A sense of direction
      2. A reason for being
   B. Spiritual achievement
      1. Believing wholeheartedly
      2. Behaving consistently
   C. Societal encouragement
      1. Fellowship
      2. Leadership

25

From Womb to Tomb

Genesis 25

The experiences of earthly life originate in the womb and terminate in the tomb. But there is much that we do not understand about man in the womb and perhaps even more that we need to know about man in his tomb, not to mention what it means to be a man in between.

   I. Man in the womb (vv. 21–26)
      A. The emotional aspect
         1. A desire expressed
         2. A prayer answered
      B. The physical aspect
         1. A sexual union
         2. A normal pregnancy
      C. The spiritual aspect
         1. The predestination of significance
         2. The predestination of separation

      3. The predestination of strength
      4. The predestination of service
   D. The personal aspect
      1. The formation of personality
      2. The demonstration of identity
      3. The intimation of hostility
   E. The moral aspect
      1. The sanctity of life
      2. The stability of the mother
      3. The viability of the children

II. Man in the tomb (vv. 1–11)
   A. Before the tomb–the time for preparation
      1. According to divine direction
         a. The position of Isaac
         b. The place of the brothers
      2. According to practical considerations
         a. Purchasing the tomb
         b. Making the will
      3. According to full participation
         a. Living an empty existence
         b. Dying "full of years"
   B. By the tomb–the time for reconciliation
      1. Family differences in the light of death
      2. Eternal issues in the light of eternity
   C. Beyond the tomb–the time for consummation
      1. Buried with his wife
      2. Gathered to his people (see Heb. 11:10)

III. Man in the middle
   A. Coming from the womb–a unique personality
      1. Abraham the management man
      2. Jacob the mystical man
      3. Esau the macho man
      4. Isaac the meditative man
   B. Living in the world–a unique opportunity

1. The manager had to trust
2. The mystic loved to manipulate
3. The macho despised the spiritual
4. The meditator tended to be fooled

C. Going to the tomb—a unique responsibility
   1. Ready or unready
   2. Forgiven or unforgiven

26
Pressure Points

Genesis 26

There is a tendency for Bible readers to place biblical characters on pedestals. This tends to divorce the reader from the truth that God is conveying in the record of his dealings with people. An honest look at Isaac's experience shows him to be a man under constant pressure. We can learn a lot from him.

I. Isaac's privileged position
   A. A sense of destiny
      1. God's power at work in his birth
      2. God's protection in evidence in his youth
      3. God's principles engrained in his family
      4. God's provision in evidence in his marriage
      5. God's purposes made clear in his manhood
   B. A sense of responsibility
      1. To discover the purpose
      2. To learn the lessons
      3. To fulfill the function

II. Isaac's pressure points
  A. Political pressure (vv. 1–6)
    1. A national disaster
    2. A predictable reaction
    3. A spiritual reminder
    4. A divine directive
  B. Psychological pressure (vv. 7–11)
    1. A potential problem
    2. An unethical society
    3. A reflex reaction
    4. A surrender of principle
    5. A growing problem
    6. A humiliating exposure
  C. Personal pressure (vv. 12–18)
    1. A successful venture
    2. An improved situation
    3. An unavoidable development
    4. A vicious action
    5. An unfortunate solution
  D. Professional pressure (vv. 19–22)
    1. Professional necessities
    2. Professional inevitabilities
    3. Professional certainties
  E. Parental pressure (vv. 34–35)
    1. The formative years of adolescence
    2. The formalized years of adulthood

III. Isaac's practical pointers
  A. Draw continually from divine resources (vv. 2, 24)
  B. Decide convincingly your proper place (v. 25)
  C. Discover constantly your potential ministry (v. 28)

27

All in the Family

Genesis 27

The family, which is God's ordained unit for society, has been experiencing difficulties of alarming proportions in recent days. Isaac's family had similar difficulties.

I. How should a family be founded?
   A. A marriage made with care (Gen. 24)
      1. Clearly defined principles
         a. Knowing the will of God
         b. Obeying the commands of God
         c. Trusting the guidance of God
      2. Clearly stated commitment
         a. The challenge to be committed
         b. The choice to make a commitment
      3. Clearly expressed love
         a. Unafraid to love
         b. Unashamed to express
   B. Children bathed in prayer (Gen. 25)
      1. Isaac's prayer of request
         a. Children are a gift from the Lord
         b. Parents are stewards of the children

2. Rebekah's prayer of anguish
   a. Insight into God's purposes
   b. Insight into her children

II. Why does a family fail?
   A. The nature of the family's failure
      1. An atmosphere of intrigue
         a. Scheming instead of supporting
         b. Lying instead of loving
         c. Competing instead of complementing
      2. An attitude of indifference
         a. To an old man's infirmity
         b. To a young man's limitations
         c. To matters of integrity
         d. To matters of decency
   B. The causes of the family's failure
      1. The father
         a. Disregarded divine revelation (25:23)
         b. Depended on natural criteria
         c. Discounted solemn oath (25:33)
         d. Displayed prejudicial attitudes (25:28)
      2. The mother
         a. Dedicated to her own ends
         b. Operated to her own advantage (Gen. 27:5)
         c. Humiliated her own husband
         d. Manipulated her own sons
      3. The sons
         a. Esau lacked a sense of priorities
         b. Jacob lacked any sense of principle

III. When will a family flourish?
   A. When the father gives the lead
   B. When the mother gives support
   C. When the children give respect
   D. When the family gives itself
   E. When the Lord gives his blessing

28

Meet the Master

Genesis 28

Throughout human history man has shown an insatiable interest in God. Innumerable efforts have been made to discover God, but not all have proved successful. The experience of Jacob at Bethel is helpful in this regard.

    I. The action of Jehovah
        A. An intervention
            1. The timing of the intervention
            2. The means of the intervention
        B. An interpretation
            1. Jehovah identifies himself
                a. The LORD
                b. The God of Abraham
                c. The God of Isaac
            2. Jehovah commits himself
                a. Purpose
                b. Provision
                c. Protection
                d. Presence

   C. An interaction
     1. The commitment of God
     2. The response of man

  II. The reaction of Jacob
    A. He made a discovery concerning:
      1. Awareness of God
      2. Awesomeness of God
      3. Access to God
    B. He made a decision:
      1. To acknowledge the authority of God
      2. To accept the blessing of God
      3. To affirm his commitment to God
        a. He named the place
        b. He raised the stone
        c. He paid the tithe

 III. The application of Jesus
    A. The intervention of incarnation
      1. Christ the way (John 1:51; 14:6)
      2. The new and living way (Heb. 10:20)
    B. The reaction of regeneration
      1. To acknowledge Christ as Lord
      2. To accept Christ as Savior
      3. To affirm position as a believer
        a. Raise a witness
        b. Name the name
        c. Give the substance

29

The School of Hard Knocks

Genesis 29

Jacob, a man of great gifts and glaring faults, was God's choice to be the father of his people. But God decided that he should be educated in the school of hard knocks.

    I. The Founder of the school (Deut. 32:8–12)
       A. The Founder's choice (vv. 8–9)
          1. His gift to the nation
          2. His gift to himself
       B. The Founder's care (v. 10)
          1. He found him
          2. He shielded him
          3. He cared for him
          4. He guarded him
       C. The Founder's challenge (vv. 11–12)
          1. Stirring up the nest
          2. Spreading out the wings

II. The curriculum of the school (Gen. 29)
   A. The lesson
     1. That God is in control (vv. 1–14)
       a. The encounter at Bethel
       b. The meeting at the well
     2. That love is supreme (vv. 15–21)
       a. The wonder of new love
       b. The waking of disciplined love
       c. The work of maturing love
     3. That you reap what you sow (vv. 22–25)
       a. Actions have consequences
       b. Consequences have final analysis
       c. Final analysis is forecast in present circumstances
     4. That every man meets his match (vv. 26–39)
       a. Deceivers will be deceived
       b. Manipulators will be manipulated
       c. Winners will be beaten
     5. That there is a limit to man's ability (vv. 31–35)
       a. Jacob couldn't make Leah happy
       b. Jacob couldn't make Rachel fertile
       c. Neither could make Jacob content
   B. The teachers
     1. People we can't appreciate
     2. The places we can't escape
     3. The problems we can't avoid
     4. The principles we can't deny
     5. The pain we can't assuage

III. The student body of the school
   A. Their goals
     1. To learn obedience
     2. To practice dependence
   B. Their grades

1. The nature of their situations
2. The quality of their responses

C. Their graduation
   1. The conclusion of their studies
   2. The commencement of postgraduate work

30

Relationships

Genesis 30

The extraordinary situation in which Jacob found himself both as family man and employee was so fraught with problems that it is no surprise that he lived in constant tension. His relationships were strained at all times. We can learn a lot from his experience.

    I. A description of relationships
       A. Relationships as reflectors of values
          1. The value I place on Deity
             a. God's attitude to people
             b. God's attitude to relationships
          2. The value I place on humanity
             a. Man the object of God's love
             b. Man the subject of God's handiwork
          3. The value I place on personality
             a. Reactions the product of relationships
             b. Responses the result of relationships
             c. Reactions the mirror of personality

4. The value I place on morality
   a. How people ought to be regarded
   b. How people ought to be treated
B. Relationships as revealers of vices
   1. Thoughts previously unthought
   2. Attitudes previously unknown
   3. Actions previously unpremeditated
C. Relationships as refiners of virtues
   1. The necessity to love
   2. The opportunity to trust
   3. The possibility to give

II. The desecration of relationships
   A. The relationships illustrated
      1. Rachel's relationships with:
         a. Leah–jealousy (v. 1), competition (v. 8)
         b. Jacob–frustration (v. 1), humiliation (v. 5)
         c. Bilhah–arrogance (v. 3)
         d. Self–vindication (v. 6)
      2. Leah's relationships with:
         a. Rachel–bitterness (v. 15)
         b. Jacob–selfish affection (v. 16)
         c. Zilpah–arrogance (v. 9)
      3. Jacob's relationships with:
         a. Rachel–anger (v. 2)
         b. Leah–indifference
         c. Laban–distrust, distaste, ambition (v. 25)
      4. Laban's relationship with Jacob–admiration, possessiveness, greed, dishonesty
   B. The relationships evaluated
      1. The psychological aspects
         a. Basic insecurities
         b. Blatant inadequacies
      2. The cultural aspects

          a. Impossible demands
          b. Intolerable pressures
       3. The spiritual aspects
          a. The way of the Lord
          b. The wickedness of the heart
          (Mark 7:20–23)

III. A design for relationships
    A. Reevaluation of cultural norms
    B. Repentance of attitudes previously condoned
    C. Recognition of spiritual imperatives
    D. Response to Holy Spirit's enabling
       (see Gal. 5:19–26)
    E. Recommitment to biblical truths

31

Settling Differences

Genesis 31

Ever since God created society, differences of opinion have proliferated. When handled correctly, they can lead to growth of understanding and relationship, but when mismanaged they can be disastrous. Jacob and Laban are a case in point.

I. The reasons differences arise
   A. The clash of personalities
      1. The competitive factor
      2. The irritant factor
      3. The threatening factor
      4. The misunderstanding factor
   B. The conflict of interests
      1. Mutually contradictory interests
      2. Mutually destructive interests
      3. Mutually exclusive interests

C. The complexity of issues
  1. Spiritual issues
     a. Jacob's sense of God's presence (v. 5)
     b. Jacob's appreciation of God's provision (v. 7)
     c. Jacob's response to God's call (v. 13)
     d. Laban's insensitivity to the above
  2. Emotional issues
     a. Jacob's sense of being cheated (v. 7)
     b. Laban's sense of being deserted (v. 43)
     c. Daughter's sense of being used (vv. 14–15)
  3. Ethical issues
     a. Laban's casual approach to agreements (v. 41)
     b. Jacob's deceitful method of departure (v. 20)
     c. Rachel's dishonest handling of property (v. 19)
  4. Practical issues
     a. The problems attending success
     b. The pressures associated with survival

II. The results differences produce
  A. The fracturing of relationships
  B. The fear of consequences
  C. The dissipation of energy
  D. The division of resources

III. The resolution differences need
  A. An honest confrontation of the issues
     1. Jacob's desire to leave
     2. Laban's determination to manipulate
  B. A straightforward statement of feelings
     1. Jacob's deep-rooted resentments (vv. 36–42)
     2. Laban's deep-rooted hurts (vv. 26–30)
  C. A united acceptance of arbitration (v. 37)

D. A common point of reference (v. 44)
   1. The place of the Lord
   2. The commitment to agree
E. A practical introduction of guidelines (v. 52)
   1. The readiness to change position
   2. The necessity to maintain ground

32

The Main Event

Genesis 32

As we have followed the tempestuous life of Jacob, we have seen many events take place, but nothing compares with the night he wrestled with God. It was his main event and must be ours.

    I. Before the event
      A. The lessons he had learned
        1. To balance human resources with divine (vv. 1–2)
          a. The divine intervention (v. 1)
          b. The significance of *maḥănāyim* (v. 2)
        2. To balance planning with praying (vv. 3–21)
          a. Projecting a suitable attitude (vv. 4–5)
          b. Taking reasonable precautions
          c. Praying sensible prayers (vv. 9–12)
            (1) Based on the promises of God
            (2) Presented in an attitude of contrition
            (3) Spoken from the depth of the heart

B. The feelings he expressed
  1. He felt ashamed (v. 10)
     a. The fact of God's grace
     b. The fact of his ingratitude
  2. He felt afraid (v. 7)
     a. His present position
     b. His immediate expectation
  3. He felt alone (v. 24)
     a. The human fear of loneliness
     b. The divine advantage in aloneness

II. The event
  A. The night of struggle
    1. Submission or self-assertion
    2. Dependence or defiance
    3. Reliance or resistance
  B. The moment of truth
    1. The limits of God's action
    2. The touch of God's power
    3. The exposure of Jacob's impotence
  C. The hour of decision
    1. I cannot do without him
    2. I will not let him go
    3. I must be blessed of God
    4. I will admit what I am
  D. The day of blessing (v. 29)

III. After the event
  A. A new identity–Israel (v. 28)
  B. A new vision of God–Peniel (v. 30)
  C. A new day of opportunity (v. 31)
  D. A new spring in his step (v. 31)

33

Handling Relationships

Genesis 33

When God told Jacob to return to his homeland, he made a detour into Esau's territory. His action demonstrates the link between spiritual principle and social obligations. (See Matt. 7:12; John 4:20; James 2:14–17.)

   I. Learning to respect relationships
      A. The measure of morality (Exod. 20:1–17)
         1. The law as moral standard
         2. The law as relational statement
         3. The law as revealer of sin
      B. The signs of spirituality (Gal. 5:19–26)
         1. The lusts of the flesh
         2. The fruit of the Spirit
      C. The means of maturity (Matt. 5:1–11)
         1. The inevitability of conflict
         2. The probability of reaction
         3. The necessity of response

II. Working to restore relationships
  A. Willingness to admit guilt
    1. The place of conscience
    2. The experience of conviction
    3. The act of confession
  B. Readiness to accept apology
    1. The temptation to self-justification
    2. The tendency to get even
    3. The tyranny of resentment
    4. The triumph of grace
  C. Openness to administer forgiveness
    1. The meaning of forgiveness
    2. The model of forgiveness
    3. The mechanics of forgiveness

III. Knowing when to restrain relationships
  A. Esau's emotional suggestion was rejected
    1. Relationships have different levels
    2. Relationships have definite limits
    3. Relationships have dangerous liabilities
  B. Jacob's judicious response was right
    1. Head must influence heart
    2. Facts must influence feelings
    3. Discernment must influence desire

34

Violence

Genesis 34

Early in human history it became apparent that corruption would be exhibited by violence. Modern times continue to give evidence of this human dilemma. The story of Dinah and her brothers illustrates the problem and demands our careful consideration.

   I. The roots of violence
     A. Political theories of violence
       1. Revolutionary–violence to overthrow injustice
       2. Reactionary–violence to maintain law and order
     B. Evolutionary theories of violence
       1. Optimistic–the values of animal aggression
       2. Pessimistic–sophisticated aggression, extinction
     C. Psychological theories of violence

      1. The inner conflict of human nature
      2. The external application producing self-destruction
   D. Cultural theories of violence
      1. The stress of cultural change
      2. The violence of self-defense
   E. Biblical theories of violence
      1. The rejection of God
      2. The substitution of self
      3. The alienation of society
      4. The violation of divine image

II. The results of violence
   A. The destructive results
      1. The destruction of human dignity
         a. The sanctity of life
         b. The finality of death
      2. The prostitution of human personality
         a. The perversion of love (vv. 1–4)
         b. The abuse of trust (vv. 24–25)
      3. The plunder of human property
         a. The right to possess
         b. The evil of dispossessing
      4. The theft of human territory
   B. The cumulative results
      1. Passionate action produces passionate reaction
         a. Love expressed illegitimately (vv. 1–3)
         b. Grief demonstrated immoderately (v. 7)
      2. Violent action invites violent reaction
         a. The violation of an individual
         b. The extermination of a people

III. The response to violence
   A. The noninvolvement of Jacob
      1. His hatred of violence (v. 30)

2. His fear of violence (v. 30)
3. His vulnerability to violence
B. The total involvement of Reuben and Levi
  1. Violence was necessary
  2. Violence was justifiable (v. 31)
C. The partial involvement of the brothers
  1. No part in the violation of human dignity
  2. Full participation in the violation of property
D. The correct attitude of believers to violence
  1. Noninvolvement?
  2. Total involvement?
  3. Partial involvement?

35

Spiritual Renewal

Genesis 35

J acob's experience at Bethel had changed his life. But many years had gone by and many events had taken place that made a return to Bethel imperative. We all need similar spiritual renewals.

I. Why is spiritual renewal necessary?
  A. Because human memory is faulty
    1. Remembering God's Word to Jacob (28:13–15)
    2. Remembering Jacob's word to God (28:20–22)
  B. Because human commitment is fickle
    1. Allegiance to Jehovah
    2. Infiltration of false gods (31:30)
  C. Because human fortunes fluctuate
    1. The simplicity of youthfulness–Bethel I
      a. Independence
      b. Opportunity

2. The complexity of mature age–Bethel II
   a. Dependents
   b. Responsibility
D. Because human lives are fleeting
   1. The passing of the older generations (35:8)
   2. The arrival of the succeeding generations (vv. 16–18)
E. Because human experiences are formidable
   1. The death of Rachel (v. 19)
   2. The deception of Reuben (v. 22)

II. How is spiritual renewal experienced?
   A. By getting back to basics (28:10–22)
      1. Rediscovering the sense of awe
      2. Rebuilding the place of sacrifice
      3. Reviewing the promises of God
      4. Restating the words of commitment
   B. By getting rid of barriers (35:14–15)
      1. Making the decision
      2. Doing the necessary

III. When is spiritual renewal possible?
   A. The renewal of daily devotions
   B. The renewal of regular worship
   C. The renewal of consistent fellowship
   D. The renewal of climactic events

36

The Bitter Root

Genesis 36

The story of Esau is full of human interest and packed with spiritual significance. Scripture strongly advises us to see in his experience warnings that should be heeded.

   I. Esau's experience
      A. He despised his birthright (Gen. 25:34)
         1. The significance of the birthright to the Israelites
            a. Specially consecrated to God (Exod. 22:29)
            b. Specially honored in the family (Gen. 49:3)
            c. Specially blessed materially (Deut. 21:17)
            d. Specially endowed spiritually (Gen. 17:6–8)

2. The insignificance of the birthright to Esau
   a. He preferred the sensual to the spiritual (Gen. 25:30)
      (1) Senses stimulate appetite
      (2) Appetites produce and preserve life
      (3) Excessive appetite is counterproductive
      (4) Spiritual values guard against excess
   b. He preferred the immediate to the ultimate (Gen. 25:32)
      (1) Living in the "here and now"
      (2) Living in the light of "there and then"
B. He disgraced his family (Gen. 26:34–35)
   1. Unholy alliances (Gen. 24:3–4)
   2. Unrestrained living (Heb. 12:16)
C. He displayed his nobility (Gen. 33:1–12)
   1. Nobility in the midst of profanity
   2. Baby in the midst of bath water
D. He desired his blessing (Heb. 12:16)
E. He disseminated his attitude
   1. The antipathy of the Edomites (Num. 20:21)
   2. The hostility of the Amalekites (Num. 14:45)
   3. The cruelty of the Temanites (Obad. 9:14)
   4. The sensuality of Herod (Mark 6:14–29)

II. Esau's example
   A. A man whom God disqualified (Gen. 25:23)
      1. The choice of God
      2. The foreknowledge of God
   B. A man who displeased God (Mal. 1:2–5)
      1. The consistency of divine displeasure
      2. The consequences of divine displeasure

III. Esau's exhortation (Heb. 12:14–17)
   A. Beware of the bitter root
      1. In the life of the individual
      2. In the experience of the community

37

A Good Kid

Genesis 37

The final chapters of Genesis zero in on the life of Joseph. His remarkable story starts with his betrayal at the age of seventeen, an event that shows clearly the qualities already present in his young life—qualities that when refined and tested, show how a good kid becomes a great man.

 I. The making of a good kid
     A. The place of principles
         1. The principle of work (v. 2)
         2. The principle of right
         3. The principle of good
         4. The principle of truth
         5. The principle of faith (vv. 5–9)
     B. The place of problems
         1. Age six (Gen. 31–33)
             a. Problems related to evading issues
             b. Problems related to facing music

    2. Age eleven (Gen. 34)
       a. Problems related to sin's wages
       b. Problems related to human violence
    3. Age sixteen (Gen. 35)
       a. Problems related to loss of loved ones
       b. Problems related to betrayal of trust
  C. The place of priorities (Gen. 35)
    1. Getting back to basics
    2. Getting rid of contradictions
    3. Getting down to business
  D. The place of pressures
    1. Peer pressure
       a. The pressure to conform
       b. The pressure to confront
       c. The pressure of contempt
    2. Parental pressure
       a. The favoritism of a fond father
       b. The disapproval of a disappointed dad
  E. The place of pain
    1. The emotional pain of rejection
    2. The psychological pain of desertion
    3. The physical pain of imprisonment
  F. The place of Providence
    1. The intricacy of the plan of God
       (Gen. 15:13)
    2. The intimacy of the presence of God
       (Acts 7:9)

II. The making of a good kid's parent
  A. Knowing God enough to make him known
  B. Loving the kid enough to let him grow
    1. Exposure to problems
    2. Experience of pressure
  C. Trusting God enough to let him lead
    1. Believing in God's perfect will
    2. Cooperating in God's perfect ways

38

The Chain of Events

Genesis 38

Human history is full of monumental events, but the monumental events are linked by apparently insignificant happenings. The importance of the unimportant is clearly seen in the chain of events involving Judah, the fourth son of Israel.

I. Looking at the links in the chain of events
   A. The importance of relationships
     1. Judah's careless approach
       a. The move from the family (v. 1)
       b. The change of environment
       c. The development of a friendship
       d. The institution of a marriage (v. 2)
       e. The establishment of a family (v. 3)
       f. The disregard of an obligation (v. 11)
       g. The misinterpretation of an event
       h. The breakdown of discipline (v. 15)
       i. The miscalculation of consequences (v. 23)

2. Er's contemptible approach (vv. 6–7)
   a. The enormity of his misdeeds
   b. The finality of God's judgment
3. Onan's carnal approach (vv. 8–10)
   a. Cultural norms
   b. Sexual desires
   c. Moral consequences
4. Tamar's calculating approach (vv. 13–26)
   a. She decided on her rights
   b. She sacrificed herself
   c. She believed the end justifies the means
   d. She covered all bases
   e. She achieved her objective
   B. The impact of reactions
1. God's reaction to Er and Onan's actions
2. Judah's reaction to God's action
   a. Misinterpreted
   b. Misplaced
   c. Mistaken
3. Tamar's reaction to Judah's action
4. Judah's reaction to Tamar's action
   a. He bared his soul
   b. He shared the blame
   c. He spared the woman

II. Learning the lessons from the chain of events
    A. The responsibility of man
1. The factors governing choices
2. The fallout following choices
    B. The sovereignty of God
1. The immensity of his power
2. The irresistibility of his intervention
   a. Jacob and not Esau
   b. Judah and not Reuben
   c. Perez and not Zerah

C. The humility of Christ—See Matthew 1
1. Tamar
2. Rahab
3. Ruth
4. Bathsheba
5. Mary
D. The universality of salvation—whosoever will may come
E. The vulnerability of the church
1. The necessity to maintain divine standards
2. The necessity of mediate divine mercy

39

Success

Genesis 39

The dictionary defines "success" as (1) a favorable outcome or result, or (2) the gaining of wealth, fame, rank, etc. God granted Joseph success in the house of Potiphar, but how closely his experience matched the popular definition should be carefully considered.

I. Nothing succeeds like success
   A. Success must be defined
      1. The objectives need clear identification
         a. The dream of a captive (37:5–10)
         b. The charge of a leader (Josh. 1:8)
         c. The ministry of a servant (Isa. 53:7–12)
      2. The criteria need careful evaluation
         a. A person, not a producer
           (Luke 12:13–21)
         b. A lover, not a loner (3 John 2–6)
   B. Success must be recognized

      1. The practical evidence (Gen. 39:2)
      2. The spiritual interpretation (v. 3)
    C. Success must be appreciated
      1. The overflow of blessing (v. 5)
      2. The increase of opportunity (v. 6)

II. Nothing seduces like success
    A. The advent of seduction
      1. The highly visible are highly vulnerable (v. 7)
      2. The highly successful are highly susceptible
      3. The highly attractive are highly attainable
    B. The attraction of seduction
      1. Conquests breed a desire for conquest
      2. Liberty produces a desire for license
      3. Opportunity invites through the door it opens
    C. The antidote to seduction (vv. 7–13)
      1. The possession of principle
      2. The statement of position
      3. The rejection of proposition
      4. The avoidance of possibility
      5. The escape from problems

III. Nothing sustains like success
    A. The sustaining power of past victories
      1. In the prison where he was held
      2. In the principles he maintained
    B. The sustaining power in difficult circumstances
      1. The external suggestion of failure
      2. The internal assurance of success
    C. The sustaining power of future goals
      1. The evaluation of the immediate in the light of the ultimate
      2. The recognition of the Lord in the work of man
      3. The appreciation of the painful in the light of the possible

40

Discouragement

Genesis 40

By the time he reached his early twenties Joseph had experienced enough discouragements to last most people a lifetime. The way he handled these situations is most enlightening for all those who suffer discouragement.

I. Some reasons for discouragement
    A. Unpleasant environment
        1. Adjacent to Potiphar's home
        2. Described as a "hole" (v. 15)
        3. Shackles and chains (Ps. 105:18)
    B. Unfair treatment
        1. Mistreated by his brothers
        2. Falsely accused by his employer's wife
        3. Unjustly condemned by his employer
        4. Forgotten by his friend (Gen. 40:23)
    C. Unending disappointment
        1. Disappointed with life
           a. Inadequate reward for effort

   b. Negligible support for goodness
   c. Apparent advantage of wickedness
  2. Disappointed with God
   a. The greatness of God's promises
   b. The smallness of God's action
  3. Disappointed with people
   a. The insensitivity of the captain (v. 4)
   b. The ingratitude of the cupbearer (v. 23)

 II. Some reactions to discouragement
  A. Some natural reactions (vv. 14–15)
   1. A touch of resentment
   2. A trace of self-pity
   3. A tendency to bargain
  B. Some practical reactions
   1. Involvement in the affairs of others
    a. A compassionate concern (v. 7)
    b. A commitment to minister (v. 8)
   2. Insistence on the sovereignty of God
    a. He gives the revelation
    b. He imparts the interpretation
   3. Inflexibility in keeping standards (vv. 12–18)
    a. Discovering the truth
    b. Telling the truth

 III. Some resources for discouragement
  A. The commitment to the Savior (Matt. 11:28–30)
   1. The breadth of the invitation
   2. The depth of the involvement
  B. The comfort of the Scriptures (Rom. 15:4)
   1. The necessity to know the Scriptures
   2. The opportunity to trust the Scriptures
  C. The communion of the Spirit (2 Cor. 13:14)
  D. The community of the saints (Heb. 10:24–25)
   1. The meeting together
   2. The ministry to each other

41

Living in Two Worlds

Genesis 41

After thirteen years of unrelenting frustration Joseph was suddenly promoted to a position of eminence in Egypt. His dream was fulfilled. It is interesting to note that it was the spiritual qualities of Joseph that led to his appointment in the secular world: a reminder that spiritual people live in two worlds.

I. The spiritual world
   A. It involves experience of the Spirit
      1. The revealing work of the Spirit (1 Cor. 1:10–14)
      2. The regenerating work of the Spirit (John 3:5–8)
   B. It involves expression of the Spirit
      1. Expression of spiritual fruit (Gal. 5:22–23)
         a. In the lifestyle of Joseph
         b. In the recognition of Pharaoh
      2. Exercise of spiritual gift (Gen. 41:16)

      a. The recognition of God's part
      b. The responsibility of man's part
    3. Explanation of spiritual truth (v. 25)
      a. God knows what he is doing
      b. Man needs to know what he's doing

II. The secular world
  A. Its principles
    1. Humanity is the center of the universe
    2. Time is the extent of experience
    3. Earth is the limit of environment
    4. Matter is the measure of value
  B. Its practices (1 John 2:15–17)
    1. Lust of the eyes–preoccupation with possession
    2. Lust of the flesh–preoccupation with passion
    3. Pride of life–preoccupation with position
  C. Its problems
    1. Discovering the truth (Gen. 41:8)
      a. The relative simplicity of the dreams
      b. The absolute certainty of the interpretation
    2. Doing what is right
      a. The plight of the lean cattle
      b. The might of the fat cattle
      c. The fight between both
    3. Directing its activities (vv. 33–34)
      a. The scarcity of leadership
      b. The difficulties of fellowship

III. The spiritual person in the secular world
  A. Intimidation by the secular world
    1. Unable to stand against it
    2. Unwilling to be different from it
    3. Unprepared to do anything for it

B. Isolation from the secular world
   1. Overwhelmed by its condition
   2. Overanxious about personal survival
   3. Overlooking spiritual opportunity
C. Infiltration of the secular world (vv. 41ff.)
   1. A clear sense of calling
   2. A consuming desire to serve
   3. A continuing state of dependence

42

Leadership

Genesis 42

The need for leadership is being stressed these days, and even a casual glance at our society shows why. The experience of Joseph as "lord of the land" in Egypt gives many helpful suggestions on the subject.

I. Why is leadership necessary?
   A. From the human perspective
      1. The immensity of physical need (41:54–55)
         a. The horror of famine
         b. The helplessness of people
      2. The prevalence of emotional depression (42:1)
         a. The immensity of the problems
         b. The scarcity of solutions

    3. The experience of spiritual guilt (vv. 21, 28)
      a. The passing of the years
      b. The pressure of the sin
    4. The bondage of natural fears (vv. 28, 35, 38)
      a. The presence of trouble
      b. The absence of answers
    5. The consequences of family breakdown
      (vv. 3, 22)
      a. The deception and suspicion
      b. The hostility and self-interest
  B. From the divine perspective
    1. The complexities of God's plan
      a. His plan for Israel
      b. His plan for Joseph
    2. The niceties of God's purposes
      a. He chose to make humans responsible
      b. He chooses to make people usable

 II. What does leadership involve?
  A. The acceptance of responsibility
    1. Required to respond to God (v. 18)
    2. Required to respond to Pharaoh (41:40)
  B. The reputation for dependability
    1. Saying what you will do
    2. Doing what you will say (41:49)
  C. The flair for creativity
    1. The ability to have a vision (41:33–36)
    2. The capability to sell a concept
  D. The development of ability
    1. The ability to communicate (41:46)
    2. The ability to motivate (42:11ff.)
    3. The ability to delegate (41:34)
    4. The ability to participate (42:6)
  E. The exercise of authority
    1. The recognition that all authority is derived
      from God

2. The consciousness that all authority may be abused by man
   a. The tendency to intimidate (vv. 6–7)
   b. The temptation to vindicate
   c. The temptation to manipulate

III. Who can exercise leadership?
   A. In a general sense, everybody leads somebody
   B. In a special sense, those who:
      1. Have a sense of calling
      2. Have identified their gifts
      3. Are willing to serve

43

It's a Changing World

Genesis 43

Life had taken some remarkable twists for Joseph and his family. The changes they experienced made considerable adjustment necessary. How they coped is instructive to us as we live in a changing world.

    I. The realities of change
        A. Change will be inevitable
            1. Natural processes ("Nae man can tether time or tide."–Robert Burns)
                a. Jacob's waning authority (cf. 42:4; 43:15)
                b. Jacob's diminishing ability (cf. 32:13; 43:11)
            2. Human actions
                a. Judah's fresh courage (cf. 37:26; 43:5)
                b. Judah's new commitment (43:9)
            3. Divine interventions
                a. Joseph's strange environment (cf. 37:12; 41:41)
                b. Joseph's new power (cf. 37:24; 43:26)

B. Change may be uncomfortable
  1. The reasons for Jacob's discomfort (43:1–14)
    a. Having to change his mind
    b. Having to relinquish control
  2. The reasons for Judah's discomfort
    (vv. 3–10)
    a. Having to change the status quo
    b. Having to change the course of events
  3. The reasons for Joseph's discomfort
    (vv. 26–34)
    a. Having to handle new opportunities
    b. Having to adjust to new situations
C. Change can be intolerable
  1. The intolerable stress of Jacob—the dread of things changing for the worse (vv. 6, 14)
  2. The intolerable stress of Joseph—the amazement that things were so good (v. 30)
D. Change should be profitable
  1. For Jacob
    a. The chance to be humbled
    b. The opportunity to trust (v. 14)
  2. For Judah
    a. The chance to face a challenge
    b. The opportunity to do some good
  3. For Joseph
    a. The chance to exercise his abilities
    b. The opportunity to show his worth

II. The reactions to change
  A. Those who see change as all bad
    1. Distrust of everything new
    2. Dislike of having to change
  B. Those who see change as all good
    1. Approval of everything novel
    2. Antagonism to everything old

C. Those who see change as both
   1. Acceptance of the inevitable
   2. Discernment of the trends
   3. Resistance of the unacceptable
D. Those who see change as under God's control
   1. The mercy of God Almighty (v. 14)
   2. The treasure of God "in your sack" (v. 23)
   3. The grace of God in blessing

44

Putting Things Right

Genesis 44

Joseph's treatment of his brothers seems at times to have been vindictive, yet underlying all his actions was a carefully thought-out plan designed to deal with the situation in which they found themselves. Deep-rooted problems rarely have simple, quick answers.

I. The things that go wrong
   A. Between family members
      1. Close contact leads to increased tension
      2. Increasing tensions produce bad attitudes
      3. Unsatisfactory attitudes prompt wrong actions
      4. Wrong actions destroy adequate relationships
      5. Inadequate relationships dismantle basic structures
   B. Between God and humans
      1. Humanity's makeup incorporates divine principles
      2. Divine principle demands human cooperation
      3. Human uncooperativeness produces sin

    4. Sin gives birth to death
    5. Death means separation from God
  C. Between believers
    1. Believers are to live corporately
    2. Corporate living requires maturity
    3. Immaturity produces division
    4. Division fractures the body

II. The things that need to be done
  A. Relationships must be evaluated realistically
    1. The lack of integrity in Israel's family
    2. The lack of reality in God's family
    3. The lack of charity in the church family
  B. Responsibility must be accepted individually
    1. The tactic of generalization
    2. The tactic of evasion
    3. The tactic of celebration
    4. The tactic of spiritualization
  C. Repentance must be undertaken genuinely
    1. The necessity of pressure
      a. Joseph's careful application of pressure
      b. The brothers' consistent evasion of issue
    2. The inevitability of pain
      a. The hurts run deep
      b. The healing necessitates cleansing
    3. The importance of purity (see 2 Cor. 7:8–13)
      a. The nature of worldly sorrow
      b. The reality of godly sorrow
    4. The place of practicalities
      a. The profession of a changed attitude
      b. The demonstration of a changed life

III. The things that can go right
  A. Families the environment of social maturity
  B. God the essence of spiritual reality
  C. Church the scene of divine activity

45

He's Alive

When Joseph appeared before his brothers alive, well, and very much in control, they were obviously very shaken. Their experience was not dissimilar to that of countless disciples who have discovered that Jesus Christ is alive, well, and very much in control.

   I. Joseph's revelation
     A. The realities of his revelation
        1. As he was, not how he used to be–he was the victim, now the vizier
        2. As he was, not how they hoped he was–he was alive, they thought he was dead
        3. As they were, not how they wished they were–they had covered up, now they were exposed
     B. The reasons for his revelation
        1. The need for reconciliation

a. Aloneness (v. 1)
   b. "Come close" (v. 4)
2. The need for education (vv. 5–8)
   a. Personal responsibility
   b. Divine sovereignty
C. The reactions to his revelation
   1. The release of pent-up emotions (v. 2)
   2. The realization of stored-up guilt (v. 3)
   3. The recognition of heaped-up blessings (vv. 17–23)
   4. The restraint of pumped-up hostilities (v. 24)
D. The results of his revelation
   1. The individual advantages
   2. The relational benefits
   3. The spiritual significance
   4. The eternal repercussions

II. Jesus' resurrection
   A. The realities of his resurrection
      1. It was consistently predicted
      2. It was thoroughly authenticated
   B. The reasons for his resurrection
      1. The need for man to be reconciled to God
      2. The need for man to be educated
   C. The reactions to his resurrection (see I.C. above)
   D. The results of his resurrection (see I.D. above)

46

The God of Surprises

Genesis 46

S keptics claim that God was manufactured by human ingenuity to meet human inadequacy—that man made God in his own image. Contemporary spiritual movements do little to counter this position by their insistence on a God who is limited to meeting human needs and satisfying human desires. The real God is surprisingly different from many human concepts.

I. The surprising purposes of God
   A. He intends to be revealed
      1. On the cosmic scale—"I am *ʾēl*" (v. 3a)
      2. On the covenant level—"the God of your father" (v. 3b)
   B. He insists on being revered
      1. As in Israel's desire for confirmation (v. 1)
      2. As in Israel's demonstration of commitment (v. 1)

II. The surprising practices of God
  A. He is the God who creates
    1. The creative initiative is his
    2. The creative capability is his
    3. The creative intention is his
  B. He is the God who communicates
    1. On the personal and intimate level–"Jacob, Jacob" (v. 2)
    2. On the relevant and effective level–"Beersheba"
    3. On the spiritual and national level–"you" (v. 4)
  C. He is the God who calculates
    1. The best person–Joseph
    2. The best place–Egypt
    3. The best position–vizier
    4. The best procedure–famine
  D. He is the God who commiserates
    1. Bringing encouragement to the fearful (v. 3)
    2. Bringing confidence to the doubtful (v. 4)

III. The surprising people of God
  A. Their customary lack of numerical superiority (v. 26)
    1. The principle of the nucleus
    2. The power of multiplication
    3. The influence of the salt
  B. Their relative lack of social acceptability (v. 34)
    1. Because they question society's standards
    2. Because they criticize society's methods
    3. Because they substitute society's objectives (see 1 Cor. 1:26–31)
  C. Their total lack of spiritual ability (Gen. 46:8)
    1. Their inability to be what they ought
    2. Their inability to forgive what they've done

     3. Their inability to do what they should (see
       1 Cor. 6:9–11)
  D. Their surprising lack of crippling inferiority
     1. The power of their witness
     2. The impact of their lives

47

Life Is a Pilgrimage

Genesis 47

When Jacob described his life, and that of his fathers, as a pilgrimage, he no doubt had in mind the nomadic lifestyle they had adopted. But a closer look at his statement shows that he meant much more. His attitude needs to be duplicated among modern Christians.

    I. Developing a pilgrim mentality
       A. Toward life (Phil. 3:20–21)
          1. Citizens of heaven
          2. Residents on earth
       B. Toward death (Heb. 11:13–16)
          1. Before death–anticipation
          2. After death–realization
       C. Toward the world (1 Peter 2:11–12)
          1. The pilgrim's warfare
          2. The pagan's welfare
       D. Toward values (Matt. 6:19–21)
          1. Earth's values are superficial
          2. Eternity's values are substantial

II. Encountering the pilgrim difficulty
   A. Difficulties common to people
      1. Shortage of resources (Gen. 47:13)
      2. Change of status (v. 17)
      3. Intervention of government (v. 20)
      4. Loss of freedom (v. 21)
      5. Imposition of restrictions (v. 24)
      6. Uncertainty of future (v. 31)
   B. Difficulties peculiar to pilgrims
      1. Maintaining objectivity (1 Peter 2:9)
      2. Fulfilling responsibility (1 Peter 2:12)
      3. Handling hostility (John 15:18–21)

III. Demonstrating the pilgrim quality
   A. The quality of dignity (v. 7)
      1. Not overwhelmed by adversity
      2. Not overawed by authority
   B. The quality of integrity (v. 9)
      1. Admitting difficulties
      2. Admitting deficiencies
   C. The quality of versatility (v. 27)
      1. The utmost importance of purpose
      2. The relative unimportance of circumstances
   D. The quality of tenacity (vv. 29–31)
      1. Knowing what you're doing (Hab. 3:17–19)
      2. Knowing where you're going

48

The Ages of Man

Genesis 48

Deathbed scenes can be horrendous. When Jacob was dying the scene was beautiful. The attitudes of those gathered around his bed and the actions of the old man demonstrated not only their healthy relationship but also how men of different ages should behave.

    I. The elderly man—the voice of the past
        A. Failing faculties
            1. The erosion of abilities (v. 1)
            2. The deterioration of memory (v. 8)
            3. The wandering of thoughts (v. 7)
            4. The loss of sight (v. 10)
        B. Residual resources
            1. The strength of determination (v. 2)
            2. The recollection of fundamentals (v. 3)
            3. The support of family (v. 1)
            4. The tenderness of love (vv. 7, 11)

   C. Crucial contributions
     1. The reminder of spiritual roots (v. 3)
     2. The recalling of spiritual promises (v. 4)
     3. The recounting of spiritual heritage (v. 15a)
     4. The rehearsing of spiritual experience
       (vv. 15–16)
     5. The relaying of spiritual blessing (v. 20)
     6. The recognition of spiritual principles (v. 14)

 II. The middle-aged man—the mainstay of the present
   A. His responsibilities
     1. Joseph as vizier
     2. Joseph as son (v. 1)
     3. Joseph as father (v. 9)
   B. His frustrations
     1. Apportioning his time
     2. Submitting to authority (v. 5)
     3. Maintaining his position (v. 19)
   C. His resources
     1. The high sense of calling (v. 9)
     2. The clear sense of enabling (v. 21)
     3. The deep sense of commitment

III. The young man—the hope of the future
   A. The opportunities of youth
     1. To gain a sense of history (v. 16)
     2. To learn the meaning of authority
     3. To catch a glimpse of destiny (v. 20)
     4. To get in touch with reality (v. 21)
   B. The temptations of youth
     1. To ignore what has already transpired
     2. To reject what has been made available
     3. To fail to prepare for what lies ahead

49

Appropriate Blessings

Genesis 49

God had promised Abraham and his seed that they would inherit the land of Canaan and through them all the nations of the earth would be blessed. Now that he is about to die, Israel gathers his sons around him and reiterates God's promise and shows in detail the part that his sons and their tribes will play in the grand plan. His words are full of surprises.

    I. Reuben—the man who was disqualified (vv. 1–4)
       A. Born to greatness (v. 3)
       B. Bound by passion (v. 4)
       C. Banished from leadership

   II. Simeon and Levi—the men who were dispersed (vv. 5–7; see Josh. 19:1–9)
       A. Unrelenting in their reactions (v. 5)
       B. Unreliable in their attitudes (v. 6)
       C. Unacceptable in their excess (v. 7)

III. Judah—the man who was distinguished (vv. 8–12)
  A. Nobility of character (43:9–10; 44:33–34)
  B. Acceptability of leadership (49:8; Num. 2:2–9)
  C. Immensity of impact (Gen. 49:10–12)
    1. Incarnational impact (v. 10)
    2. International impact (Rev. 5:1–5)

IV. Joseph—the man who was different
  (Gen. 49:22–26)
  A. The secret of his fruitfulness (v. 22)
    1. Roots by the spring (v. 22)
    2. Branches over the wall (see John 15)
  B. The secret of his strength (Gen. 49:23–24)
    1. Steadiness under pressure
    2. Strength through dependence
  C. The secret of his blessings (vv. 25–26)
    1. Following the Shepherd
    2. Building on the Rock
    3. Accepting the help
    4. Receiving the blessing
      a. Meteorological
      b. Mineral
      c. Marital
      d. Maternal
      e. Material

50

When Things Get Worse

Genesis 50

The contrast between the funerals of Jacob and Joseph clearly illustrates the changing circumstances of Joseph and the children of Israel in Egypt. Joseph's behavior, in his final days, is a great example of how Christians should behave when things get worse.

    I. Joseph's statement of faith
       A. The intellectual aspect of faith
          1. Faith that God's person is unique (v. 19)
          2. Faith that God's purposes are good (v. 20)
          3. Faith that God's promises are sure (v. 24)
       B. The relational aspect of faith
          1. Relating to God personally
          2. Relating to purposes emotionally
          3. Relating to promises psychologically
       C. The crucial aspect of faith
          1. The choice to believe
          2. The commitment to believe

D. The continual aspect of faith
   1. Going on believing despite circumstances
   2. Going on believing to the end

II. Joseph's symbol of hope
  A. A statement of his own hope (v. 25)
  B. A symbol of hope to the oppressed
  C. A sign of hope to the homeless

III. Joseph's show of love
  A. The faithfulness of love
    1. Faithful unto death (v. 1)
    2. Faithful to oath (v. 5)
  B. The fondness of love
    1. Fondness sensitive to frailty (vv. 17–19)
    2. Fondness sensitive to fear
  C. The forgiveness of love
    1. God's place in forgiveness (v. 19)
    2. Man's role in forgiving (v. 21)

Part 2

Let's Do It God's Way

51

Who Needs the Ten Commandments?

Exodus 20:1-17

Two things stand out in modern Western society—a sense of disorientation and confusion, and a distaste for authority. That the two things are connected is not always acknowledged, but a study of the Ten Commandments will show this is the case.

I. How we got the Ten Commandments
    A. The Abrahamic Covenant (Gen. 12:1–3)
    B. The Egyptian captivity
    C. The Mosaic exodus (Exod. 14:1–31)
    D. The renewed covenant (Exod. 19:1–6)
    E. The divine instructions (Exod. 10:1–17)
        1. How to love God (Deut. 6:5)
        2. How to love people (Deut. 10:19;
           Lev. 19:18)
        3. How to live well (Deut. 6:2, 18)
        4. How to be God's people (Exod. 19:5–6)

II. Significance of the Ten Commandments?
   A. Society is like an orchestra
      1. Individual instruments
      2. Harmonious relationship
      3. Piece to be performed
   B. Do they have significance for believers?
      1. "We are not under law but under grace!" (Rom. 6:15)
      2. "By observing the law no one will be justified" (Gal. 2:16)
      3. Paul is addressing Judaizers
      4. What Christ said (Matt. 5:17–18)
      5. What Paul said (Rom. 8:4)
   C. Do they have significance for unbelievers?
      1. "The Ten Commandments are too simplistic"
      2. "Everything is relative–there are no absolutes"
      3. "I have to be free to be me"
      4. "The Ten Commandments are outdated and outmoded"
      5. Answer–they apply nevertheless
         a. Creation ethics predate covenant
         b. Moral similarities in differing cultures
         c. Universality of God's promise (Jer. 31:31–34; Isa. 2:2–4)

III. How should we apply the Ten Commandments?
   A. Like a compass to give direction
   B. Like a bridge to exercise restraint
   C. Like a thermometer to measure devotion
   D. Like a mirror to see reality
   E. Like a guardian to bring us to Christ

52

Who Is Number One?

Exodus 20:3

The Lord introduced his rules for living with a dramatic statement—"You shall have no other gods before me!" This meant he was placing himself above and beyond all human speculations about deities and establishing his claim to be number one.

I. The competition—"other gods"
   A. Man's religious instinct
      1. "Man is by his constitution a religious animal."—Edmund Burke
      2. "A seed of religion is planted in all men." —John Calvin
      3. Romans 1:18–20; Psalm 19:1–4
   B. Man's perverted ingenuity
      1. Observation of natural forces
      2. Identification of deities
      3. Polytheism of Canaanites, etc.

4. "Canaanite religion . . . no pretty picture . . . extraordinarily debasing form of paganism."
   –John Bright

II. The commandment–"No other gods"
   A. The revelation
      1. The Lord is one (Deut. 6:4)
         a. Unique–greater than Egyptian gods
         b. Unity–unlike contradictory pagan pantheon
      2. The Lord is God (Exod. 20:1–2)
         a. Speaks with authority
         b. Acts in supremacy
      3. The Lord is gracious (Exod. 20:2)
         a. Brought you out
         b. Freed from slavery
   B. The reasons
      1. The problem of syncretism
         a. Local deities for each town
         b. Personal deities transferred in marriages
      2. The problem of sensualism
         a. The nature of paganism
         b. The nature of man

III. The Choice–"Choose you this day . . ."
   (Josh. 24:15; 1 Kings 18:21)
   A. The initial decision
      1. Who is Lord?
      2. What does he desire?
      3. What does he deserve?
      4. What does he demand?
      5. Whom do you serve?
   B. The continual evaluation
      1. Is he Lord?
      2. Do I serve him faithfully?
      3. Do I love him deeply?
      4. Do I worship him exclusively?

53

Making God in Man's Image

Exodus 20:4-6

Thomas Watson, preaching in the seventeenth century, said in the first commandment worshiping a false God is forbidden. In this (the second commandment) worshiping the true God in a false manner is forbidden. God's concern is to protect his people from the repercussions of such error.

I. The denunciations of idolatry
   A. What God had to say (Exod. 20:4-6)
      1. Don't represent the Creator by the created
      2. Don't render to anything that which belongs to God
      3. Don't miscalculate God's reactions–jealous-zeal for righteousness
      4. Don't forget God's grace
   B. What the prophets had to say
      1. The powerlessness of idols (Isa. 46:1-7; Jer. 10:1-5)
      2. The meaninglessness of idols (Isa. 44:9-20)

C. What the apostles had to say
   1. Idolatry is to be studiously avoided
      (1 Cor. 10:14)
   2. Idolatry is to be carefully evaluated
      (1 Cor. 10:19–21)
   3. Idolatry is to be continually recognized
      (Col. 3:5; 1 Thess. 1:9)

II. The dangers of idolatry
   A. Idolatry makes means into ends
      1. Initially intended to aid
      2. Subsequently serves to hinder
   B. Idolatry substitutes things for the Person
      1. Evil things that he hates
      2. Good things that he made
   C. Idolatry places imagination above revelation
      1. Metal images are consequence of mental
         images (Packer)
      2. Mental images are consequence of fallen
         imagination
   D. Idolatry imposes limits on divine transcen-
      dence
      1. Heaven of heavens cannot contain him
      2. Created things cannot adequately represent
         him
   E. Idolatry places man in control of God
      1. God is what man makes him
      2. God is where man puts him
   F. Idolatry fashions God in the current style
      1. Jehovah becomes Baal
      2. The covenant relationship becomes a Near
         Eastern cult
   G. Idolatry detracts from God's chosen image
      1. Man made in God's image (Gen. 1:27)
      2. Christ sent in God's image (John 14:1–7)

III. The destructiveness of idolatry (Hos. 8:4)
   A. The destruction of church life—when means matter more than ends
   B. The destruction of ministry—when serving the Lord is superior to the Lord we serve
   C. The destruction of reality—when fantasy takes the place of truth
   D. The destruction of reverence—when God fits in our box
   E. The destruction of significance—when we are the sum totality
   F. The destruction of distinctiveness—when we are indistinguishable from secular society

54

Using God for My Own Ends

Exodus 20:7

At first sight the third commandment seems to be banning profanity. But careful study shows that much more is at stake. Juliet said, "What's in a name?"–implying "nothing." But she was mistaken.

I. What's in a name?
   A. The question in a general sense
      1. Name–reputation (Phil. 2:9; Gen. 11:4; Prov. 22:1)
      2. Name–character
         a. Parents' wishes–sons of Jacob (Gen. 30)
         b. Prophetic statement (Luke 1:31; Matt. 16:17–18)
         c. Personality changes (Gen. 35:10)
      3. Name–authority
         a. God's naming of creation (Gen. 1)
         b. Adam's naming of living creatures

B. The question as it relates to "The name of the
   Lord"
   1. God chose to reveal his name
      a. To Abram (Gen. 17:1)
      b. In contrast to pagans who named their
         gods
   2. God made himself knowable
      a. He introduced himself (Exod. 6:2–3)
      b. He revealed his identity
   3. God invited intimacy–N.B. Jacob
      (Gen. 32:29)
      a. He portrayed his character
         (Exod. 3:13–14)
      b. He promised his presence
   4. God provides protection (Ps. 20:1;
      Prov. 18:10)
      a. His name speaks of his power
      b. He is president and resident (e.g., David;
         see 1 Sam. 17:34, 46)
   5. God offers salvation
      a. Through faith in his name (1 Cor. 6:11)
      b. The effects of salvation
   6. God permits identification
      a. The privilege (Acts 9:15)
      b. The pain (Acts 9:16)

II. How do we "take the name in vain"?
   A. Misuse in Old Testament times
      1. Using the name in magical incantations–the
         experience of Balaam (Num. 22, 24)
      2. The taking of oaths lightly–the careless use
         of the name (Lev. 19:12); the casual calling
         on the name (1 Kings 2:23)
      3. The dichotomy of profession and perfor-
         mance–God's people serving God's enemies
         (Lev. 20:1–3)

B. Misuse in our day
1. Making a name for myself when professing his name (Acts 8:9–25)
2. Praying in his name for my exclusive benefit (James 4:3)
3. Calling on his name without committing to his control (e.g., baptism, marriage)
4. Ministering in his name for less than acceptable motives (Acts 19:13–16)
5. Using his name carelessly, without regard to its significance

55

This Is the Day

Exodus 20:1-8

Work and leisure are integral parts of life. The fourth commandment shows how profoundly important they are.

    I. Remember the Sabbath day

       A. The inauguration of the Sabbath

         1. Introduced in the wilderness
(Exod. 16:22–30)

         2. Confirmed at Sinai (Exod. 20:8–11)

           a. The significance of work (Exod. 20:9)

           b. The necessity of rest

             (1) No going out (Exod. 16:29)

             (2) No farming (Exod. 34:21)

             (3) No fire (Exod. 35:3)

             (4) No burdens (Jer. 17:21–22)

             (5) No exceptions–strangers, animals,
land

    B. The explanation of the Sabbath
      1. God's rest at creation (Exod. 20:11)–a humanitarian gift (Lev. 25:1–17)
      2. God's deliverance in Egypt (Deut. 5:15)–an invitation to worship (Ps. 92:1–15)
      3. God's offer of a covenant (Exod. 31:12–17)– an opportunity for obedience (Exod. 20:8)
    C. The desecration of the Sabbath
      1. Business as usual in Nehemiah's time (Neh. 13:15–22)
        a. Disinterest in worship
        b. Disobedience in lifestyle
      2. Obsession with externals in Christ's time (Mark 3:1–5)
        a. Concern for the letter of the law
        b. Unconcern for the spirit of the law
    D. The clarification of the Sabbath
      1. Christ's actions
        a. He worshiped on the Sabbath (Luke 4:16)
        b. He healed on the Sabbath (Luke 6:1–11)
      2. Christ's announcements
        a. He was fulfilling the law (Matt. 5:17)
        b. He was Lord of the Sabbath (Luke 6:5)
        c. Sabbath was made for man (Mark 2:27)

 II. From Sabbath day to Sunday
    A. A transitional period
      1. The first day of the week (Acts 20:7; 1 Cor. 16:1)
        a. Resurrection
        b. Appearances
        c. Pentecost
      2. The council at Jerusalem (Acts 15:22–28)
      3. The Lord's Day (Rev. 1:10)
    B. A theological principle

    1. Was Sabbath transferred to another day?
    2. Was Sabbath no longer binding?
  C. A traditional problem
    1. Sabbatarianism?
    2. Antinomianism?
    3. Discipleship
      a. Every day is special (Ps. 118:22–23; Matt. 21:42; Acts 4:11)
      b. Sunday is even more special

56

Life in the Family

Exodus 20:12

To honor father and mother presupposes we know them, appreciate their significance, and are afforded opportunities of expressing our respect. This requires, of course, a lasting, intimate relationship in a suitable environment—we call it the family.

I. The changing family
   A. The family in biblical times
      1. The biblical concept of clan and household
         a. Joshua 7:16–18
         b. Luke 2:4
      2. Advantages of this system
         a. Economic survival—"that you may live long"
         b. Emotional stability—"may be well with you"
            (1) Extended family
            (2) Roots and identity (e.g., names)
            (3) Household experience

        c. Educational structure
          (1) Parent-child dialogue
            (e.g., Exod. 12:26; 13:14)
          (2) Family conversions (e.g., John 4:53;
            Acts 10:33–34)
  B. The family in modern times
    1. The changes
      a. From extended to nuclear
      b. From hierarchy to individuality
      c. From stability to mobility
      d. From traditional to novelty
    2. The causes
      a. Urbanization (e.g., move from family
        farm)
      b. Industrialization (e.g., move from family
        to factory)
      c. Communication (e.g., move from famil-
        ial to media)
    3. The consequences
      a. Better housing, health, education
      b. Deteriorating relationships
      c. Emotional disorders
      d. Confusion concerning values
      e. Marital and family fragmentation
  C. The family of the future
    1. Pessimistic view—"The family is near the
      point of complete extinction"
    2. Optimistic view—"Turbulence of tomorrow
      will drive people deeper"
    3. Mediating view—"The family will break up,
      shatter, and come together again in weird
      and novel ways"; "future shock"

II. The unchanging factors
  A. The family's divine origin
    1. e.g., Adam, Noah, Abram, Israel
    2. See Ephesians 3:15

B. The family's divine order
1. Father and mother honored
   a. Literally "to state one is deserving of respect, attention, and obedience" (N.B. Isa. 29:13)
   b. Father's part in protection, direction, and provision
   c. Mother's part in bringing to birth, care, nurture
2. Father and mother to be honorable
   a. A sense of divine calling and privilege
   b. A sense of divine accountability and responsibility
C. The family's divine opportunity
1. To start off doing it his way (N.B. Matt. 10:32–39)
2. To seek a new start where necessary
3. To assist those for whom neither is possible

57

The Sanctity of Human Life

Exodus 20:13

"Thou shalt not kill" appears, on the surface, to be an easy-to-understand commandment, but careful study will show how far-reaching it really is.

I. The significance of this law
   A. Its meaning
      1. Not a blanket prohibition against taking human life (e.g., Exod. 21:12–17; Num. 35:6–21; Deut. 20:10–15)
      2. Prohibition of acts of premeditation, vengeance, and malice
   B. Its rationale
      1. Man is made in the image of God (Gen 9:6)
         a. Part of animal kingdom
         b. Capable of conceptual thought
         c. Participates in divine creative purpose

   d. Possesses moral sensitivity
   e. Able to communicate with God, and be communicated to by God
   f. Has eternal, immortal dimension
  2. To destroy man is to challenge divine intent
  3. To murder is to abrogate divine authority
  4. To end human life is to despise divine evaluation

II. The relevance of this law
 A. The abortion issue
  1. Recent "liberalization" (e.g., U.S.S.R., 1920; U.S.A., 1967, 1973)
  2. What is the status of the fetus?
   a. Biblical information (Exod. 20:22–25; Jer. 1:4–5; Ps. 139:13–15; Luke 1:31–32; 41–44)
   b. Medical information–development, viability, etc.
   c. A person? Fully human? Subhuman? Potentially human?
  3. What about the mother?
   a. Her physical, emotional, spiritual well-being
   b. Rights of the unborn versus rights of the living
  4. What is the answer?
   a. Can we countenance abortion on demand?
   b. Can we ban abortion, period?
   c. Can we uphold sanctity of life of both living and unborn?
 B. The suicide issue
  1. Heroic, romantic, pessimistic suicide
  2. Unacceptable because:
   a. Usurps divine prerogatives

        b. Destroys immeasurably valuable entity
        c. Insults humanity at large
  C. The capital punishment issue
    1. Capital punishment is biblically acceptable (e.g., Gen. 9:6; Rom. 13:1–5)
    2. Element of punishment (fitting the crime), deterrence, restoration
    3. But open to abuse
  D. The war issue
    1. The "just war" doctrine
    2. The nuclear buildup
    3. The destruction by man of his own stewardship

III. The importance of this law (Matt. 5:20–26)
  A. Christ's commitment to divine law
  B. His rejection of human accretions
  C. His exposure of motive
  D. His eternal perspective

58

Preserving the Sanctity of Marriage

Exodus 20:14

It is clear from both the prophetic (Jer. 5:7–9) and apostolic (1 Cor. 5:1–5) ministries, not to mention the ministry of Christ himself (Matt. 5:27–32), that ancient cultures had severe problems with sexual immorality. God's obvious concern about this is related to his commitment to the sanctity of marriage. God's Word in this regard needs to be heeded today.

    I. The curse of adultery
        A. Adultery defies God
            1. The example of Joseph (Gen. 39:9)
            2. The confession of David (Ps. 51:3–4)
        B. Adultery destroys families
            1. God's commitment to the family (Deut. 6:2)
            2. Adultery warranted the death penalty! (Deut. 22:22)
        C. Adultery defiles marriage

    1. Marriage is exclusive (Gen. 2:24)
    2. Marriage is permanent
  D. Adultery denies love
    1. Love's dimensions (Rom. 13:8–10)
    2. Love's application–loving your spouse and children?
  E. Adultery derides faithfulness
    1. The place of covenant (Prov. 2:16–17)
    2. The destruction of trust (Mal. 2:13–16)
  F. Adultery degrades people
    1. Physical damage (Rom. 1:24)
    2. Emotional scarring–self-worth?
    3. Communal impact (1 Cor. 5:6)
    4. Spiritual implications (1 Cor. 6:18–20)

II. The causes of adultery
  A. Uncertain standards
    1. Divine principles?
    2. Contemporary mores?
  B. Unrestrained sexuality
    1. The God-given sex drive
    2. The need for limits
  C. Unfulfilled desires
    1. Unsatisfactory marriages
    2. Unlimited opportunities
  D. Undisciplined lifestyle
    1. Adultery of the mind (Matt. 5:28)
    2. Adultery of the eyes
  E. Unconfessed sin
    1. Recognizing lust (Mark 7:20–23)
    2. Refusing to deal with it (James 1:13–15)

III. The cure of adultery
  A. Preventative
    1. Agree with God

    2. Grow in grace (Col. 3:1–10; Gal. 5:19–25)
    3. Guard yourself in the Spirit (Mal. 2:16; Matt. 5:27–30)
  B. Remedial
    1. A repentant spirit (John 8:1–11)
    2. A loving Savior (John 8:11)
    3. A caring community (1 Cor. 6:9–11)
    4. A forgiving family (e.g., Hosea)

59

Handling Property Properly

Exodus 20:15

George Gallup, Jr., said recently, "It is ironic that while religion in America is growing in popularity, morality is declining." The *Wall Street Journal* reported recently that a poll showed no difference in attitudes between "churched" and "unchurched" people with regard to cheating on expense accounts and tax reporting.

I. The shapes and sizes of stealing
  A. Stealing from humans
    1. Depriving a person of property is stealing
      a. Property as necessity (1 Tim. 6:6–8; Deut. 24:6–13)
      b. Property as a right (Exod. 20:17)
      c. Property as a trust (Ps. 24:1)
    2. Depriving a person of liberty is stealing
      a. Persons as God's servants (Lev. 25:55)
      b. Denying freedom to be what God intended (Deut. 24:7)

3. Depriving a person of dignity is stealing
   a. Destroying a reputation
   b. Degrading a name (e.g., Acts 19:25–27)
   c. Denying a person justice (Isa. 10:1–3)
4. Depriving a person of opportunity is stealing
   a. The businessman's opportunity to do business (Titus 2:10)
   b. The government's opportunity to govern (Luke 20:25)
   c. The poor man's opportunity to survive (Deut. 24:14–15)
   d. The suffering man's opportunity to recover (Deut. 15:7–11)

B. Stealing from God
   1. Contradictory behavior robs God of credibility (Jer. 7:1–11; Luke 19:45–46)
      a. Powerful profession
      b. Pitiful performance
   2. Refusing tithes and offerings robs God of honor (Mal. 3:8–10)
      a. Tithes and offerings belong to the Lord (Lev. 27:30)
         (1) The annual tithe (Deut. 14:22–27)
         (2) The three-yearly tithe (Deut. 14:28–29)
         (3) The offerings for sacrifice (Deut. 12:6)
         (4) The special offerings (Exod. 35:4)
      b. Failing to give is keeping what is God's
         (1) First-rate stinginess (Neh. 13:10; Eccles. 5:13)
         (2) Second-rate sacrifice (Mal. 1:6–14)
         (3) Third-rate motives (Matt. 6:2; Acts 5:1–11)

II. The dangers and damage of stealing
   A. Stealing may land you in trouble with the law
   B. Stealing will ruin your relations with others
   C. Stealing leads to deception of lies
   D. Stealing shrivels the one who does it
   E. Stealing places extra burdens on others
   F. Stealing hinders the work of God

III. The blessings and beauty of quitting stealing
   (Eph. 4:28)
   A. The blessings of repentance
   B. The blessings of restitution
   C. The blessings of hard work
   D. The blessings of beneficial production
   E. The blessings of giving
   F. The blessings of being a blessing

60

Speaking the Truth

Exodus 20:16

Our judicial system requires witnesses to tell the truth, the whole truth, and nothing but the truth. Failure to do so is called perjury, which is a crime bearing severe penalties. God, who is far more committed to truth than man, expects us to tell the truth, too.

    I. God's prohibition against lying
        A. The struggle of God against the devil
           (John 8:42–47)
           1. The Father of righteousness
           2. The father of lies
        B. The struggle of good against evil
           1. God's creation–"good" (Gen. 1)
           2. The devil's commitment–"destruction"
             (John 10:10)
        C. The struggle of truth against delusion
           (2 Cor. 4:4–6)
           1. The blinding of delusion
           2. The eye-opening of truth

D. The struggle of righteousness against sin
  1. Righteousness in the law (Deut. 19:15–21)
  2. Righteousness in the life (Prov. 14:25; 25:8)

II. Man's propensity toward lying
  A. Man's propensity to lie to himself
    1. Man is conscious of himself
    2. Man has opinions of himself (Rom. 12:3)
    3. Man can lie to himself (Rom. 1:28–32)
  B. Man's propensity to lie to God (Acts 5:1–11)
    1. A desire to find favor with God
    2. An unwillingness to relate adequately to God
  C. Man's propensity to lie to his neighbor
    1. The destructive lie (Matt. 26:59–60)
      a. Malicious intent (e.g., Gen. 39:16–18)
      b. Erroneous content
    2. The defensive lie (Luke 22:54–62)
      a. The fear of exposure
      b. The compounding of guilt
    3. The defective lie
      a. The lies of carelessness
      b. The lies of boastfulness
      c. The lies of silence
      d. The lies of half-truth
    4. The deceptive lie
      a. Designed to deceive
      b. Intended to defeat

III. Christianity's provision to avoid lying (Eph. 4:15–32)
  A. Learning the truth (vv. 20–24)
    1. Recognize the truth in Jesus
    2. Reject lies opposed to truth
    3. Receive new life in Christ
    4. Resolve to live in righteousness

B. Loving the truth
   1. Because it is unloving to lie (v. 15)
   2. Because it is antisocial to lie (v. 25)
   3. Because it is counterproductive to lie (vv. 29, 31)
   4. Because it is opposed to the Spirit to lie (v. 30)
C. Living the truth (1 Peter 3:15–17)
   1. Living the truth in word
   2. Living the truth in deed

61

Forbidden Fruit

Exodus 20:17

The tenth commandment differs from the other nine in that they deal specifically with actions, while it deals with an attitude—covetousness. But it is clear that actions originate with attitudes (see Gen. 3:6 and 1 Tim. 6:10).

I. What does covetousness mean?
   A. God-given desires
      1. The desire to acquire
      2. The desire to succeed
      3. The desire to produce
      4. The desire to progress
   B. God-given delights
      1. The delights of creation (Gen. 2:9)
      2. The delights of love (Song of Sol. 1:1–4)
      3. The delights of truth (Ps. 19:10)
      4. The delights of gifts (1 Cor. 12:31; 14:39)
   C. God-given denials
      1. Denying the right to desire excessively

  a. When need and greed become confused
     (Jer. 6:13; 8:10; Ezek. 33:13–32)
  b. When competition leads to destruction
  2. Denying the right to desire illegitimately
     a. Some fruit is forbidden (Gen. 2:15–17)
     b. Some areas are off-limits (Josh. 7:21)
  3. Denying the right to desire exploitatively
     (2 Peter 2:3)
     a. Viewing people as objects
     b. Using people for personal advantage
  4. Denying the right to desire exclusively
     (Luke 12:13–21)
     a. When personal gain becomes all-important
     b. When all-important things become in-
        significant
  D. What then is covetousness?
  1. The attitude that worships desire
  2. The attitude that pursues delight
  3. The attitude that denies denial

II. What does covetousness do?
  A. It leads to dishonesty and injustice
  1. David and Bathsheba (2 Sam. 11:1–27)
  2. Jezebel and Naboth (1 Kings 21:1–29)
  B. It creates insatiable demands
  1. An inbuilt tendency (Mark 7:22)
  2. An expanding economy
  3. A calculated manipulation
  C. It confuses moral judgment
  1. An idol of personal gain (Eph. 5:3–5)
  2. A deifying of material things (Luke 16:14)
  3. A worshiping of self at the expense of oth-
     ers (2 Tim. 3:2)

III. What should we do about covetousness?
  A. We need to search our hearts

    1. Am I greedy for position, prestige, praise, possessions?

    2. Am I lusting after off-limits people and things?

    3. Am I motivated primarily by self-interest and personal gain?

B. We need to confess our sins

    1. Do I recognize greed from need?

    2. Do I acknowledge greed is sin? (Isa. 57:15–19)

C. We need to adjust our lifestyle

    1. The joy of sharing

    2. The peace of contentment (Heb. 13:5)

Cassette tapes of the sermons preached from the outlines in this book are available from

TELLING THE TRUTH
P.O. Box 11
Brookfield, WI 53005